MAKING OF A CHAMPION

...there was a champion called David

YINKA AKINTUNDE

MAKING OF A CHAMPION

...there was a champion called David

YINKA AKINTUNDE

RESOURCE HOUSE LTD
LONDON

MAKING OF A CHAMPION

Copyright@ Yinka Akintunde 2014

All Rights Reserved

ISBN : 978-0-9568267-2-5

No part of this book may be reproduced in any form by photocopying or by any electronic or mechanical means, including information storage or retrieval systems without permission in writing from both the copyright owner and the publisher of this book.

First Published 2014 by

RESOURCE HOUSE LTD
resourcehouse@ymail.com
info@diademministries.org
www.diademministries.org

All Bible quotations have been taken from the New King James Version of the Bible, unless otherwise indicated in the text. 'KJV' refers to King James Version. 'Amp' refers to Amplified bible. 'NIV' refers to New International Version. 'NLT' refers to New Living Translation.

Printed for Resource House

Contents

Introduction

1. KINGDOM CHAMPION / 11
Made not Elected
Born Again to reign

2. CHOSEN CHAMPION / 21
Chosen from the Lots

3. ANOINTED TO REIGN / 29
Anointed Within for Conquest
Anointed Upon for Performance

4. SERVING CHAMPION / 40
Family Business
Gifted but Given

5. CHAMPION OF FAITH AND WISDOM / 50
Faith for Supernatural Help
Ideas for Victories

6. BAKED IN FURNACE / 67
Refiner's Fire
Enemy's Fire

7. CHAMPION IN LOVE / 75
Loving God

- CONTENTS -

8. HUNTED BUT WINNING / 87
Hunted by Memories
Hunted with Offence

9. PRIEST AND KING / 101
Much Business

10. WINNING HERE AND THERE / 116
The Now Life

11. WINNING LEGACIES / 124
Generational Blessing
Leader of Company

12. MADE STRONG / 129
When I am Weak

Acknowledgement

To the Godhead in person of the Father, Son and the Holy Spirit, through Whom all wisdom and inspiration flow be all glory and thanksgiving.

My precious wife and lovely kids, Diadem Church members, Dele Popoola, Tunde Fayombo and every other person and institution who have been a blessing to my person and ministry over time.

God bless you all.

Introduction

Irrespective of the in-born abilities, gifting or talents in whatever vocation of life you are endowed with, champions are made eventually and not born as it were. We live in a world of potentials and limitless potentials for that matter, yet we live in a world of many underachievers living and dying with untapped potentials and unused resources.

Being a champion goes beyond achievements, it is a personality, a way of life and a conscious and subconscious make-up of the inner personality which comes up whenever there is a trophy to lay claim to.

Champions have peculiar ways of thinking, pattern of response to deploy towards challenges. They have regime of trainings to engage in and discipline to be exercised in that bring out the ultimate champions in them.

Anyone can win once in a blue moon by luck or happenstance, but champions deliberately go for winning and get it done against all odds. Champions can seemingly lose a battle here and there but they never lose the war eventually.

To champions, the only final destination is winning and winning again and again.

Beneath every glory are stories, behind every mask of championship is a human personality; Elijah was described as a man of like passion but a winning man as well. [1.1]

1.1 - *James 5:17*

Every worthy champion will tell you in retrospect that the sweetness of victory is in the sweat-ness of becoming that victorious person which they are and not just the accolades and glory which follow the victories they have. The process of becoming never leaves the winning one the same, the mould is formed and the winning inevitable in anyway.

It is God's ultimate pleasure to make an all-conquering one out of each of his children, but it takes a believer submitting self to the necessary moulding for the champion in one to come out. Nothing is left to chance by heaven when it comes to the destiny of a saint; destinies are orchestrated for good; but it's worthy of a saint to dance to the tune of divine orchestration so that the champion heaven has in mind can evolve.

There is no honorary champion in life; all champions paid the necessary price for the greater one in them to come out. It is therefore my desire and prayer that as you go through this material you will discover the missing link and re-align yourself to whatever moulding is laid before you by God.

There was a champion in the camp of natural Israel some few millennia ago whose name was David. He was such a champion among champions that the flag of Israel as a nation today simply bears the Star of David. Enormous was the winning streak of this great champ that even Jesus is said to be sitting on the throne of David as the Loin of the tribe of Judah. It is the life of this same David we will examine briefly in this book that we may see the

- INTRODUCTION -

pros and cons of the making of a kingdom champion, so we can line up our lives for absolute conquest too.

It is my prayer that generation after you will still be carrying the flag of your star simply by reason of depth and legacies of your far reaching conquests while on this on earth. I see the all-conquering champion in you coming out in Jesus precious name.

Chapter One

KINGDOM CHAMPION

Every kingdom is a reflection of the King's essence, greatness, might and splendour; same with the kingdom of God. It is not a kingdom of weaklings and losers; it is the kingdom of the almighty all-conquering God. Believers aren't champions on the account of their personal might and abilities; we are champions because we are in the champion's camp. We represent a God that has never and will never lose a battle.

Every nation sends the best they can muster to represent them in whatever competitive event at the global stage, same with the kingdom of God. You were sent down here because you are simply the best of your kind. This is not one of those flatteries but an eternal truth, or how else would it have been, seeing you are called the kingdom ambassador [1.2]. No wise nation sends forth a foolish ambassador; no strong nation sends forth a weakling as an ambassador. The accession into such office through the ranks and experience would have brought out the good and desirable qualities in them even if hidden initially.

Kingdom First

In the kingdom of God, no champion is allowed to be a champion for the fun of championship, neither is anyone allowed to be a champion for vain glory. It is contrary to

1.2 - *2 Corinthians 5:19*

the kingdom concept for the champions themselves to be the centre of the show. Nothing else is allowed to take the centre stage but the King and his kingdom. Once winning is a mere show of strength, defeat is inevitable.

David understood this concept as a teenage army recruit, who was not selected for the battle at the valley of Elah. Saul the king and all his men of war with the elders and cabinet did not grasp the fact that the battle with the Philistine was not a mere battle of armies of nations in conflict, but a battle between the Philistines and the army of the Lord. It is an internal state of being, it is a mind-set; a godly outlook of things with the kingdom priority perspective.

Goliath saw the battle at hand as a battle between him and some lesser men; a battle between his strong nation and another nation for territorial dominance. Saul and his men also saw the war as such and so for them it was Goliath versus the army of "Israel" **[1.3]**. In reality, heaven didn't see the battle as such; the battle was between light and darkness, between Goliath and the army of the Lord. Once the right man came with the right perspective of the kingdom of God, it was easy for the unseen army of the kingdom to be dispatched for supernatural assistance.

The champion in you might not come out until you come out of seeing life challenges from racial, national and other perennial points of view. God won't bless or lift a Christian because he or she belongs to a race or nationality, not even because of the gender. For a saint, life challenges go beyond those mundane and shallow

1.3 - *1 Samuel 17:8-10*

outlooks; it is simply a challenge of kingdoms. The kingdom of darkness versus kingdom of light; the kingdom of heaven versus the kingdom of this world: God's versus Satan's.

Many people are Christians until someone of rival political party shows up in their domain with a contrary political view. The default setting of many Christians is to quickly ignore all the kingdom principles of brotherhood the moment tribal or racial war of attrition begins. To such people, they are first Americans or British or Chinese or South African or Nigerians before they are Christians. They are first democrats or republicans before they are Christians. They are first black, white or mixed race before they are Christians.

David said to Saul and his men in clear terms, that the battle could not be won because someone defiled the army of a particular nationality, race, party or tribe. The battle was about to be won simply and only because Goliath defiled the army of the Lord [1.4].

Kingdom champions are first kingdom representatives and ambassadors before any other denominator comes into the equation. Every conquest must be such that the crown will be laid at the feet of the king of our kingdom, not at the feet of your tribal chief or group association or national flag. It is high time believers started crossing racial, tribal, gender and national borders and boundaries to win for God's kingdom and the kingdom alone.

1.4 - *1 Samuel 17:26*

Made not Elected

Democratic ethos and processes are good for the purpose of civil rule but not beyond that. Democracy has no place in the personal evolvement for destiny and victory in personal conflicts we face in life. You can't wait till the whole world vote you in and agree with you before you let the greater one within you evolve. The reality is that at no time will the majority be on your side as it were; even you yourself won't be on your side initially at time when it comes to serious issue of bringing the champion out of you, but what has to be done has to be done in any case.

The big battle that brought David into public consciousness was the battle at the valley of Elah where Goliath was defeated by David. Up until Goliath's head went off his neck by the hand of David, at no time was David the popular choice to fight such a daunting battle. As a young recruit in the army, he was sent back in the day of battle to "wait for his time and turn"**[1.5]**. The sad reality is that at no time will majority really think it's your time; everyone thinks it's their own time and not yours. David was the eighth son of his father, and it was only the first three, by popular vote, that made the cut in his father's house to the battle. Going by human calculations and permutations it would have taken forever for the champion in the young man to come out if there was even any at all. Rejected and overlooked stones by men have always been important cornerstones of the kingdom of God at last.

Are you refused and rejected of men and so feeling bad and down? Before you start crying and looking for

1.5 - *1 Samuel 17:15*

someone to conduct a special deliverance service for you or before you finally count yourself out of the championship race of life, consider David the kingdom champion and rejoice for being in a good company. Kingdom champions are not initially popular with men because as far as the East is to the West, so is God's way and choice to the way and choice of men.

The only one who eventually gave David a chance was Saul the king, and as far as who was who at the valley of Elah was concerned on that fateful day, Saul was the main man in the camp of Israel. He was the king with overriding authority. Always remember that God is the king over all kings. His vote is the vital and indispensable vote needed in the championship of life. Once secured, it will compel the majority vote you need eventually by favour or by force. You can imagine the looks in David's brothers' faces that day; talk less of the looks on their friends' faces that really never cared about David anyway. To them he was a forward teenager who was always telling tales of fighting lions and bears with bare hands around town.

Every man in the battlefield that day had a uniform and armour to show off as belonging to a company of warrior. The only credential David had was a story of having been made to fight killers like Goliath at the backside of nowhere before. My friend, see the rejection and refusal as part and parcel of the process of being made. It was the sending back of David from the war job that landed him in the shepherd's job; and it was at the shepherd's job he learnt rising up to the occasion in the name of the Lord even when the odds looked so much against him. All it took David to land the job of taking on Goliath was the testimonial of killing a lion and bear that rose against him on the field. You can imagine Saul raising his brow towards David's brothers to confirm if the stories were true and how reluctantly they would have nodded their heads in unison and affirmation even though they hated doing so.

Favour is not mere currying of likeness by whomever, but for whoever is relevant on your path to be compelled by higher power to do you good even when they hate doing so.

The rejection is part of being made, the refusal is part of being made, the rising and attacking lions and bears are parts of being made. Remove those unpleasant experiences from the resume of a champion what you will have left is a shell of uniform and armour wielding cowards who have fought nothing or can fight nothing of great significance. Don't see yourself as having it too hard in life, rather, know deep down that to be made a champion is more than being born as one. It is a tortuous and convoluted process.

Thrones are Ascended not Inherited
Kingdom champions are pace setters and trail blazers. Unfamiliar territories are the familiar terrains for them. The law of antecedent is not necessarily unbreakable for champions.

Kingdom thrones are ascended and not merely inherited;

ascension comes at a price and not given as a gift. Even as an heir, you will be placed under tutelage of ascension till the time appointed by the father or else it will be called a mutiny **[1.6]**.

In ascension, timing is very crucial. David was anointed to be king around the age of fifteen against the law of inheritance as he was not a descendant of Saul the king by blood. He didn't sit on the first throne till fifteen years later when he became the king of Judah and another seven years and six months to become the overall king of Israel. This made his making time twenty two and a half years to become the king of Israel which he was anointed to be as a teenage boy. Every effort by association of women singers to win him public vote and crown him earlier than the set time was met with vicious envy and attack by a demon infested king. The best he could get out of it was to be chased out of the city and palace with eventual refugee status taken in the wilderness. In this kingdom, every short cut will make the journey longer, and may in fact cut short the reign of life. David understood this concept and so bid his time till he sensed that God had established his throne and kingdom at His own timing. Many designated champions in the kingdom are grinding mills in the court of the unsaved today due to impatience. My prayer is that whatever you have lost to impatience, may you gain back from now on through the mercy of God in Jesus precious name.

For all kingdom champions, winning is deliberate, calculated and in increasing order till the perfect day but of significant note it is to know that deliberate winning

1.6 - Galatians 4:1

requires deliberate and calculated steps. Kingdom champions are not impatient and rash in steps taking. However, their patience borders on temperance and not just mere sitting down doing nothing. David won many battles as a king by striking at the right time, yet he learnt waiting for the right time while ascending the throne or prosecuting the battles.

He defeated the Philistines at Baal-Perazim and Rephaim through the virtue of patience; waiting for the right time to strike **[1.7]**.

When Absalom led an insurgence to dethrone David, he took the young man out through same virtue of patience. He didn't sit tight in Zipon to get killed; he instead vacated the throne and bided his time again in the mountains until God presented him the season of recovery. I pray this moment will be your own season of recovery too. It was inherent in him that thrones are ascended and not grabbed by scheming and evil plots in this kingdom. Kingdom champions don't scheme their leaders out of place, they don't join in the petty competition of pulling others down in order to rise. David knew his ascension to the throne will be harbingered by Saul's departure at his own time through the hand of God, not by killing him pre-maturely with impatient ambition of man **[1.8]**.

Who knows, if David had been in a hurry and had killed Saul because Saul was under divine judgement, maybe Absalom the son of David too would have dethroned him successfully seeing he too was being judged of heaven at

1.7 - 2 Samuel 5:8-25; *1.8* - 1 Samuel 26:9-10

that time of the insurgence in his kingdom several years later.

No height of significance can be ascended hurriedly; the steeper the slope, the higher the height and the more patience is needed in ascension.

May you see virtue in patience and give it a place as you ascend your throne as a champion which you are.

Born Again to Reign
The whole concept of new birth is the manifestation of the conquest of the son of God, Jesus, on behalf of mankind as our all winning prince. To be born again is to be born away from the wicked and gripping hand of sin, Satan and spiritual death which had held humanity captive since the fall of Adam. The kingdom of darkness seemed to have had the last say in human affairs until our champion showed up as Christ Jesus. He lived above sin and yet died for sin; he went down into the headquarters of darkness beneath the earth and there he destroyed principalities and powers of darkness. To crown up his triumph, he rose again on the third day never to die again. It was then he became the first born from the dead or in other words, the first "born again" one among men. He is the first fruit of the Kingdom conquest through mankind.

All champions in this kingdom are ultimately taking after our prince and king, Jesus, who was significantly, mirrored in David the king

One common denominator to them both is their commitment, zeal and single minded allegiance to the kingdom of our God. Jesus quoted David verbatim severally while on earth. One of the significant one is that, he was a kingdom minded champion that had been consumed by the zeal or passion of God's house or kingdom **[1.9]**.

Kingdom champions are kingdom minded all the way. They champion the kingdom cause above every other issue first, and then the champions in them in other areas of life start showing forth as a result.

May the champion in you not be buried in the field of self and personal aggrandisement in the precious name of Jesus Christ. Amen.

***1.9** - Psalm 69:9; John 2:17*

Chapter Two

CHOSEN CHAMPION

Every kingdom champion is chosen for such purpose in his or her generation. When we say chosen, people always think of someone specially called into maybe the fivefold ministry but that is not the case at all. Every believer is called and chosen out of the lot in the world to be a champion in his or her own rightful place.

All kingdom champions have the sense of being called and chosen to win; they believe in something special about themselves and truly something is special about us all **[2.1]**.

That innermost reality of being specially chosen for victory is what always helps champions to see any set back or seeming defeat as a passing through phase which shall surely pass away. Just like a pilot had been trained to know that no matter how long or fast, taxing on ground is not the ultimate journey for an aircraft; it is built for flight, and heights, not runways or even hangers.

Chosen from the Lots

David, like a true champion he was, understood the fact that there were lots of better qualified people out there before God in his sovereign mercy chose him to be a

2.1 - *1 Peter 2:9-10*

captain over his people. This is the first question that must be settled in the mind of anyone who wants to shine in the kingdom of God. No matter your apportioned lot, there are always better qualified people God could have given. This mind set should then rid you of arrogance and pride that come with a sense of entitlement, and instead fill you with a sense of gratitude and thanksgiving all the days of your life **[2.2]**.

The news broken to David by God's prophet, Nathan, before he made this profound prayer of thanksgiving should have made any self-chosen and self-made man so bitter and feel humiliated to the point of possibly punishing the prophet for such a message. If David had had ego problem, being bluntly refused a place in the annals of history as the one who built the best temple of all time is enough to get him upset with man and God. David had blood in his hand not just because he killed Uriah the Hittite for selfish a purpose, David also had blood in his hand also because he fought God's battle against the enemies of God for the preservation of the people of God and the glory of God's kingdom. For a hand trained by God to battle to then be refused his moment of glory in building the temple sounds unfair in human language. For a champion who knew he was chosen among many qualified lots, it was just another wise divine verdict from an all-knowing God who could never be wrong.

Chosen champions can do anything for their master; they are not so caught up in PR as to forget the one who chose them. When the ark was being brought to Jerusalem,

2.2 - *2 Samuel 7:17-22*

David the champion danced before the ark vigorously, not minding what mockery will come from the politically correct armies of the day. One of such was David's wife and Saul's daughter, Micah. She saw no reason for such an elaborate dance from a king. "What will the foreign dignitaries and press think" she must have thought. She grew up in royalty and had never seen her dad, the king or any of the ranks in the royal family engaged in such a public display of emotions in the name of dancing before the Lord. She couldn't hold the shame of such an uncultured dance before God by a man chosen by God, but David's simple explanation was that the chosen can do anything for God and his kingdom no matter the mockery of the world **[2.3]**.

God will elevate you, he will bring you to public consciousness, you shall be reckoned with as a champion in your vocation; but don't be caught up in the "show biz" and political correctness bug of your generation. Stand as one raised by God for his kingdom and truth, don't court popularity and fame at the expense of the Kingdom of God. You may be a career person, a sport personality, a musician, a business man or a ministry man or woman; don't be too big in your own eye than the kingdom that raised you. Many people were raised and given platforms of expression in Church, they identified with Christ and his truth openly until wealth and fame came. They suddenly became too sophisticated to be seen with faith groups and Church matters; like Demas, they have loved this present world suddenly **[2.4]**. It's high time to re-trace your steps to your roots if you are one of such and

2.3 - *2 Samuel 6:20-23;* ***2.4*** - *2 Timothy 4:10*

reading this book right now. Come back home and lift up the name and kingdom of HE who raised you up.

True champions are not deserters but loyalists to death.

Preferred by Heaven

Child of God, may I say that you are the preferred one, a stone rejected of men but preferred by the God of heaven. You are not going to be favoured, you have been favoured already of God; all you need is appropriating the favour on earth. David's three older brothers were among the rank and file that couldn't face Goliath. How did a seventeen year old David sum up courage to do so? The answer is simple: David knew he was preferred by heaven. His three older brothers might have been chosen by the army chief, but David knew what God said through Samuel few months before then **[2.5]**.

It was not that God didn't chose David's brothers including Eliab the oldest, it was that God refused them. Whatever criteria of grace and mercy were applied, they fell short of them.

The fact that others tried and fail does not mean you will fail too; you simply might be preferred for the assignment. David's brothers were not refused from joining the Lord's army but they were refused the captainship of God's inheritance. Motivational speaking will tell you that if others can do it, you can do it too. Friend, it sounds good but it's not true. Others might be chosen and preferred for it, but you might not; none of us is chosen for everything and everywhere. Your job is to find out and know what you have been chosen, preferred

2.5 - *1 Samuel 16:6-10*

and favoured for, and be a champion therein. Kingdom champions are not out to prove the wrong points of being better than others, they simply ride on the wings of divine preference in their own territory and shinning becomes inevitable. Your favour is in the place of your preference, where you have been preferred by heaven. Everything will come in line to do you good therein eventually.

Chosen for a Reason
True champions are pilgrims of purpose, it's not enough to be great in strength, massive in number and all conquering in pursuits; it is sufficiently better to know the essence of any given might and strength. When Saul was commanded of God to battle with the Amalekites and destroy everything, he saw no reason to do the latter as long as the battle was won. For God, the battle was not just about winning another laurel; it was a battle of purpose **[2.6]**. Might and ability will definitely be abused once the concept of purpose is removed. Being anointed is for a purpose, gifts and talents are given for specific purposes, pastoring a large church is for a purpose. Most of what Christians see as achievements are really not meant to be achievements but platforms in pursuit of kingdom purpose(s). They are platforms for God to pass something significant across to the world; to edify and prepare the body of Christ further towards the coming back of the Lord.

Samson was a popular and a hugely anointed fellow, but as far as he was concerned, the whole power game was

2.6 - *1 Samuel 15:1-3*

just to catch fun with. He married whoever he liked, dated anyone, slept anywhere and ate or drank whatever. Whereas there was a vow of purpose on his head for his generation, and that was from the Lord **[2.7]**.

Kingdom champions don't fight like blind horses; they don't even get involved in certain battles of attrition being fought by worldly men and women. They are focused on their specific assignments and callings because those are where their winnings are guaranteed.

David was a champion in delivering God's people because that was the essence of his choice and calling. He was ever winning because all the battles he fought were to liberate God's people; either from the curse of a rejected Saul, from other invading nations or from a separatist within the kingdom such as Absalom. The battles were within the scope of the race set before him and so he kept winning. When we stay on track, nothing can befall us.

Chosen for a Season
No one is allowed to reign here on earth for ever in this dispensation; our reigning here for now is for a reason and a season. As long as we live in time, our reigning is time-tied and must therefore be timely as well. There must therefore be a sense of urgency within every pilgrim of purpose; we don't have forever to fulfil and finish our assignment. No time must be given to frivolities and no time for unproductive ventures. David started looking after family business as a teenage boy; he was already a winning warrior at seventeen.

2.7 - *Judges 13:3-5*

Kingdom champions don't invest major time on minor issues or vice versa. Give the bulk of your time to discovering, training and dispatching the champion in you for conquests.

David knew that opportunity to kill Goliath may be once in a lifetime and so he took the chance with both hands, when the time and chance orchestrated by heaven presented it to him. Time and chance are seasonal in collision, they are like massive waves of sea for surfers, and they don't collide too many times. You need to recognise and seize the moment. There are opportunities in time of challenges, there are opportunities in time of victories as well, don't let any just slip away.

Time of failure has its own benefits no matter how small and bitter. It could be a wakeup call not to ever fail again. It could be an opportunity to see your vulnerability and make proper and prompt adjustments to prevent mortal failure ahead. When others around you fail, it is not a time to jump on social media and be dissecting them; it could be a time for you to learn and get wiser. It is wise to learn from other peoples' fall than to comment and still be as vulnerable as they were. Saul was mortally wounded and invariably killed by an archer who shot an arrow through his chariot. Instead of David to be overjoyed in the opportunity to become a king, he saw a deficiency in the army he would eventually lead. He must have gone to review the syllabus of training and recruitment in Israel's army and saw that they were not trained in such art of warfare. The moment he became the king, one of his first ordinances was to fortify himself with archers who could shoot arrows with both hands! **[2.8]**.

When you realise how much time you have infested and lost in the past to what does not really matter in life, you then will sit down to plan and execute a recovery programme without looking back. It is not enough to feel bad and sober about your loss. Do whatever you can to recover and buy back what is left of your time **[2.9]**. The word of God said this is wisdom.

Finally on this note, kingdom champions know their own time will come eventually, they don't envy others whose times and seasons have come, neither do they scheme them out of the setting. David never for once thought of killing the heir apparent, Jonathan in case Saul died suddenly and the people of Israel follow the law of natural succession. He never knew that Jonathan would die with Saul on the same day but he knew that at His own time, God would work out his enthronement in his own perfect way.

I pray for you today that your season will be sweet and deliver all the peaceable goods and fruits of righteousness it carries for you to reign in Jesus precious name.

2.8 - *2 Samuel 1:17-18, 1 Chronicles 12:1-3;* *2.9* - *Ephesians 5: 15-16*

Chapter Three
ANOINTED TO REIGN

GOD FACTOR

All through the adventures of David, we saw a man that was winning because God made him win. The God factor in the making of every kingdom champion can't be over emphasised. A strong will to win is not sufficient in making a kingdom champion. Pharaoh and the host of Egypt had a very resolute will to have dived into the unknown path in the belly of the Red Sea. But there was a divine presence the sea saw with children of Israel before it opened up for them to pass through **[3.1]**. Same could not be said of the host of Egypt; for except the Lord watch over the city, watchmen wake in vain. Mere military training and desire not to be defeated was not enough to bring down Goliath or the host of the Philistines.

God must have been there to slay him with whatever weapon the anointed threw at him, no matter how ridiculously small it was. Even Goliath himself was surprised at and had disdain for David coming at him with a sling and some stones. It was insulting enough to send a young lad with no intimidating body build, experience or a track record of a warrior to take on him. Much more insulting was the fact that the would-be deliverer of Israel had no armour of a man who is ready for serious business of fighting **[3.2]**.

3.1 - *Psalm 114:1-7;* *3.2* - *1 Samuel 17:42-44*

Goliath had been reading and flaunting his own resume and the expected personal requirements for any challenger before Saul and the whole army of Israel for forty days, and so afraid were they, that no one bothered applying for the task of taking on him. Then came a lad who had been anointed by God few months ahead for reigning and who had started a walk with God on a personal level for that matter. The little but supernatural exploits in David's resume pointed at the presence of God and so the door for further exploits opened for him because he couldn't be kept quiet **[3.3]**.

Let the redeemed of the Lord say so, David was not ashamed to bring God into the matter, and so God was not ashamed to join the matter. Don't be ashamed to bring God into your matter, others may not believe in God or may not see the relevance of God in whatever they are passing through; your case as a kingdom champion must be different. Read out your resume with God as David did, say to Goliath that your God will bring him down with you seeing the salvation of the Lord now. Let the sea see and acknowledge the God you carry around in you and on you, it will soon part. God is truly the Supreme Being high above all, yet he stooped low to kill a lion, a bear and a Goliath. When you are not too proud, timid or ashamed to look up, the most high won't be too busy to stoop down for your sake. Bring God into your health, marriage, career, education, finances and every area of your life; see him helping you win over and over again **[3.4]**.

3.3 - *1 Samuel 17:45-47;* **3.4** - *2 Corinthians 2:14*

David didn't lay all the responsibilities at the feet of God; neither did he shy away from laying at God's feet the glory due to his name when the results showed up. When the lion and the bear came for the lamb, it was David who ran after both and snatched the lamb; it was him that smote the lion and the bear. He took responsibility as and when necessary and allowed God to do His own part. It is very needful to know that the anointing is not a substitute for taking personal responsibilities; yet the anointing can't be substituted for in any way. Champions who involve God in their conquests also get involved. They don't fold their hands lazying around because God is involved. They chase the lions and the bears; they snatch the lamb and smite whatever needs to be smitten.

The manifestation and conquest of Christ Jesus simply as God working through man showed us that co-operating with the divine is the way out for mankind. Man can't do it alone and God won't do it alone even though he can do anything **[3.5]**. Total emancipation of mankind is the work of God in man as we take responsibilities.

Anointed Within for Conquest
God is a spirit, he relates with mankind as such; He is not a white man with white hair sitting up somewhere with a big stick looking for who to knock on the head. God's ultimate plan is to have a place within His people, living in them as the sweet anointing within their human spirits. Much more than anywhere, the battles of life are mostly fought within us; this is why the ark must be

3.5 - Acts 10:38

within us lest the host of the wicked take over there. So conscious was David of the presence of God within him that he cried bitterly for God not to take divine presence of the anointing from within him when he once erred **[3.6]**. Until God conquers us within and dominates our inside through his holy anointing, the struggle on the outside will continue. Our conquest without on the earth is a direct function of how much we are dominated by heaven within. It is the flood of heaven within us that quenches the rage of hell in the outside world for us. God anoints us within as champions for two reasons:

(1)   Anointed Within for Strength:

Our God is strong and mighty, so we, His kingdom representatives can't afford to be weaklings. God does not mind picking us up in our weakness and mostly that is what he does. At the same time, God won't want to leave us in our weakness. He therefore puts the holy anointing of His Holy Spirit within us to strengthen us. Every Christian is in a race and is a soldier, and so every Christian is expected to win and not faint or give up in the championship race and battles of life. Winning requires strength, and extra strength for that matter. Everyone who participates in a marathon has strength to start; but only those who have strength to finish stand any chance of winning. Life can really sap us and suck our inner fortitude; the way out is the anointing within. Not only will we be given strength, our strength gets renewed as well by the sweet anointing within us **[3.7]**.

David understood the place of strength within so much

3.6 - *Psalm 51:10-11;* *3.7* - *Ephesians 3:13-16*

that he was speaking from his renewed spirit to his soul not to faint. Fainting is easier and cheaper than standing, giving up is cheaper than holding on. In like manner, so is fainting costlier than standing and giving up also costlier than holding on. Every investment into life can be easily lost through fainting and giving up, whereas a little more strength from within, then you will see the glory behind the curtain of your challenges.

(2) Anointed Within for Light:

In the beginning, God created heavens and the earth and He made a distinction between light and darkness. There is no midway therein. Kingdom champions are champions of light all the way. God is light and in Him is no darkness at all; every inheritance of conquest He therefore has for us are loaded up for us in light **[3.8]**. We need light to approach and get our blessings kept in light; two can only walk together in agreement.

Essentially, all life's challenges are challenges against the forces of darkness in one form or the other, it therefore takes light within to fight a good fight and come out triumphant. God anoints us with His sweet Holy spirit in the inside, so that we can know 'who', 'what', 'where', 'how' and 'when' of our conquests. We are anointed within to know who we are, who we belong to, who is for us and who is against us in the championship of life **[3.9]**. As you read and listen to the word of God in various forms, the Holy Spirit's anointing within you helps you grasp the person of God and the reality of His kingdom. Beyond the empirical world, you know the

3.8 - Colossians 1:12; *3.9* - 1 John 2:20-21

reality of the things of the spirit from the inside and start relating as such. God gave us our natural senses for the outer world but spiritual senses are activated within us by the anointing within to know the things of God. Kingdom champions don't discard but can't just rely on their natural senses in dealing with life. Resident within the natural senses are the capacities for doubt, fear and unbelief along with other vices and flaws with limitations in the first Adam. The essence of the anointing within is to show and teach us against these limitations of the natural man so we can be lightened within for exploits without **[3.10]**. David knew how to pass through troops and leap over walls, so that bows of iron were broken by his hand because the anointing within him taught him how to wage wars and his finger to battle **[3.11]**. The anointing within trains us not to buckle in by shining the light of victory in our inside when confronted with challenges of darkness and despair all around us.

The anointing within us is the centre of divine guidance as to what to do, where to go and when to do such and such. The anointing within is more than mere hearing a voice or seeing a vision; it is a total package of divine guidance. Champions necessarily are not listening for voices; they are ready for guidance from within whichever way God chooses to do it. People who strictly tie divine guidance to dreams or voices can be easily swayed by the devil. The scripture did not say as many as hear voices or dream dreams are the sons of God but as many as are led by the spirit of God which is the anointing within us.

3.10 - *1 John 2:27;* ***3.11*** - *2Sam 22:30-35*

God leads in so many ways. The assignment of a champion is to develop an intimacy of one's own spirit with the presence of the Holy Spirit within, which includes communications on either way. Guidance becomes automatic and unlaboured when needed if intimacy has been developed when there seemed to be no need for guidance at all. It is needful to develop a communication pathway with the Holy Spirit within when there is no hyper-emotional situation to be-cloud your judgement and dilute receptive ability. David was so sure of the formula of intimacy that he said it was the only thing he would desire and seek after all his days **[3.12]**. He was so sure of the veracity of divine guidance that he said in the time of trouble, he knew he would be kept and hid in the right place. When you are busy doing the right things in time of peace, it is easy to be kept in the right place of safety in time of war. Winning in life is not just about fighting but also about being kept from hurt. We live in a hurtful world filled with many injurious individuals. There is a place of being hidden by God as and when needful. Living in the buffer zone of the kingdom while the wicked rages and the world suffers is a blessing.

Anointed Upon for Performance

God was introduced to us as a performer all over the bible. In the beginning He performed when darkness and voidness was rampaging the then created earth. In like manner, God wants His kingdom champions to be performers. Men and women with results and not mere

3.12 - *Psalm 27:4-5*

tellers of stories and givers of excuses. The whole host of Israel were busy explaining and complaining about Goliath until a performer showed up in David. He woke the whole nation up on how to do it when he brought down the head of Goliath of Gat. God wants you to have results, He wants His word to work in your hand, in your finance, home, career, business and everything you lay your hands upon to do. Nobody goes to the war of the king at his own personal expense; the king of the kingdom pays for the battle. The king supplies the arms and whatever victual is needed to prosecute the war successfully. In like manner, God does not want you to go about doing it all by yourself; He places His mighty anointing on us that we might deliver. David was first of all anointed before any other quality showed up in him as a champion **[3.13]**. David was anointed for the race ahead; he was anointed for the wars ahead, and he was anointed for the tasks ahead. The difference between David and the rest was the anointing upon him. It was meant for conquests and could never fail to deliver as ordained. That was the anointing on Samson with which he destroyed the Philistines. That still was the anointing on Moses with which he took Israel out of Egypt. It was the same anointing on Joshua with which he divided Canaan for God's people as their eternal inheritance.

It is dangerous for Christians to just be full of dry theories and principles void of the power of God, assuming that the gospel is just some good news because it sounds right and sweet. No matter how promising and motivating it sounds, it only becomes the gospel of the

3.13 - *1 Samuel 16:13*

kingdom when the one proclaiming it has the anointing of the spirit of God on them to proclaim **[3.14]**. It is the gospel or the good news because it is anointed, not just because it sounds good. Take the anointing away from the gospel, what is left will be entrapment of deceits which will expose champions to defeat and ridicule at the end.

Anointing Upon as Covering
Champions are exposed to all manners of attacks and assaults of the wicked simply because of who they are and what they stand for. Saul, the son of Kish and the first king of Israel probably wouldn't have run into problems as much as he did if he were not a king. Saul would likely not be a target of attack if he was just a mere business man minding his own business and making money at the back side of somewhere. Being the point man made him the target to which the most vicious attack of hell was pointed; and yet he knew it not. Jesus said we shall be hated of men for his name's sake, simply because we belong to him. Yes, simply because you refuse either to cave in or accept defeat as your fate pitches you against formidable onslaughts: but be of good cheers. The anointing of the Holy Spirit is a covering upon us **[3.15]**.

Even when Saul was out of sync with God, David refused to touch him because he knew no one touches the anointed and be guilt free. To be anointed is to be made a god among men, placed in class above molestations of the wicked. It takes ignorance for gods to start dying and suffering like mere men. David understood the covering

3.14 - Isaiah 61:1; *3.15* - Psalm 105:12-15

power of the anointing so well that he lamented how Saul could just be killed like he was not anointed **[3.16]**. It astonished David because he knew how the anointing had delivered him when it looked like he was already cornered and outnumbered. Kingdom champions are not ordinary mere men; they can't and must not be regarding to themselves as masses like mere men **[3.17]**. Kingdom champions are gods, they are meant to manifest the big God who resides in and upon them as the greater one which is greater than all the challenges of their days. The anointing upon you is a covering from demonic and all hierarchy of evil spirits' attacks. It is a covering from diabolical attacks of the wicked occult world; it is a covering from hatred and attack of men and women with evil missions and intentions towards us who believe.

Holy Oil

The anointing of the Holy Ghost is, figuratively, the holy oil of God which sets the champions apart for God and for Him alone. They are set beyond and shielded from the wagging tongues of men. I have seen vicious attacks from the world and from their friends within the Church against truly anointed champions but never once have they prevailed. No one can prevail over people carrying God around in their inside **[3.18]**. God sets His own kingdom champions apart, not for defeat or shame, but for conquests upon conquests and for glory.

Activate the Blessing

The anointing of the Holy Spirit on kingdom champions

3.16 - 2 Samuel 1:21; *3.17* - Psalm 82:5-6; *3.18* - Psalm 89:19-37 is like holy oil, poured to lubricate and activate the blessings in the blessing wherewith we have been blessed. The following precious kingdom promises are activated when we discern the anointing:

I. Establishment in all you do by the hand of God.
II. Unfailing strength through the arm of God.
III. Freedom from enslavement by the wicked.
IV. Freedom from afflictions by the wicked.
V. God's beating down of all foes that rise up against you.
VI. Divine judgement on them that hate you.
VII. God's faithfulness and mercy constantly working for you.
VIII. Supernatural exaltation for you.
IX. Far reaching influence in your sphere of pursuit.
X. Speedy answer to your prayers.
XI. Heights beyond natural ascension.
XII. Mercy as a covering over your life.

It is therefore your responsibility not to let your head lack ointment, keep the oil fresh and flowing through fellowship with God by His word and the Holy Ghost.

I see rivers of oil ever flowing in your life, in Jesus precious name.

Chapter Four

SERVING CHAMPION

Kingdom champions are called to be kingdom servants; they are called unto the loyal service of their King's kingdom here on earth. If there is no mission to be accomplished, there wouldn't have been any need for the kingdom of heaven to set up an embassy here on earth. The Church is the operational base of the kingdom of God on earth.

The first man in God's likeness was set in dominion here on earth on behalf of heaven so as to keep the earth from decadence again. The first king on the earth was Adam. He was not enthroned for the fun of enthronement; he wasn't just set in such a great splendour and with such great abilities for the fun of showcasing. The first kingdom representative on earth was set in dominion for service purpose. To dominate, subdue and replenish are active words. He was a man set to do something, not just to fester in biological reproduction **[4.1]**. The created earth before the recreation of the earth and placement of man therein as landlord went into gross darkness and voidness because no one was in charge. When dominion is relinquished, darkness spirals out of control to consume whatever is on ground. In the course of dispensations from Adam to Christ, God sent various champions such as Noah, Abraham, Moses, Joshua and the judges -

4.1 - *Gen. 1:28*

including Gideon, Samson and Deborah. They were all servants of the kingdom of God here on earth. Once serving the kingdom of God becomes secondary to the kingdom champions, retirement becomes the only option available to heaven. Eli and his household of unborn generations were retired the moment serving God became a secondary issue to the cravings for flesh and pleasure. From Samuel, the priest-prophet, to the kings and then prophets that served as arrow heads of the kingdom till the day of Jesus Christ, all kingdom champions were set and sent to serve the kingdom of the ultimate king, even God.

"As the father sent me so sent I you", Jesus said of us the royal priesthood champions. The father sent Jesus to serve in order to bring out the great champion in him and today the serving lamb has transformed into the glorious lion of the Judah's tribe. In like manner, we are sent of Christ to serve so that our glorious place in the kingdom can be apportioned to us **[4.2]**. Your championship position is ever guaranteed in service; your kingdom appointment for reigning and your sumptuous feeding and drinking at the kingdom table are all tied to your service level. Jesus just said so in the referenced passage above.

Family Business
When David was sent back home from the army, the responsibility of looking after the family business became his next line of duty **[4.3]**. He didn't allow the disappointment of being sent back to rob him of his

4.2 - Luke 22:25-39; 4.3 - 1 Samuel 17:12-15

responsibility to his biological family. He didn't use that as a platform for idleness and irresponsibility. Champions don't become irresponsible and idle because one issue is pending and needs sorting out in their lives. Many people stop being responsible and start following the idlers on the street because they have not gotten the kind of job they want. Champions don't behave that way. Some even stop living because they have not been able to relocate to a particular place they desire. They become so irresponsible and idle that their very lives start falling apart right before their own eyes. Champions don't give up living and destiny pursuits simply because they have not been able to get married as they so desire. God expects His champions to be men and women of responsibilities, first at home and then anywhere else. The introduction of mankind on the earth was through a family structure. The acceptance of sinners into the kingdom of God after forgiveness is said to be admittance into the membership of the family of God. These underscore the importance of being integrated and responsible in our family, whether biological, as by birth or by adoption. Kingdom champions think of their families first, they are not rash in taking steps in case it would affect the family integrity. They do as much as they could to be a value adding and not value depleting member of the family. The family of man, woman and children is not a western idea, it is God's idea. Probably David did it to make his dad happy, but he did it anyway. It was in the course of looking after his father's sheep he knew how to stand up against oppression and destruction **[4.4]**. Most likely this was where he wrote his

4.4 - *1 Samuel 17:34-35*

most famous psalm, Psalm 23 too. Psalm 23 was the anthropomorphism painting God as the shepherd who would look after him just as he was looking after the family sheep too. Psalm 23 is probably the most popular passage of the whole bible. Even unbelievers recite it when shoving becomes pushing in the fierce battle of life.

David's service to the family cause was not just towards his father but even his brothers [4.5]. The hostility of David's brothers towards him when he proposed to take on Goliath painted a picture of a not too rosy kindred spirit. Nevertheless, when his dad asked him to go check on them and give them sustenance and gifts for their bosses, David did not protest in malice, neither did he start reciting how they had treated him badly earlier.

Jesse still had four older sons before David who were also not in the battle but they weren't made of champions' material. He probably could not trust them with family welfare errands. David could have gone a few days on his own frolic without seeking out his brothers and return home to avoid putting his life at risk in the battle front. He could have lied to their dad that he couldn't get to the camp of Israel because the battlefront was too hot.

The opportunity to take on Goliath and receive the best trophy came as David ran a family errand for his father to check on his brothers. Many champion skills in you will only evolve as you serve your family. Many opportunities will only show up when your family welfare becomes your errand. Kingdom champions don't ostracise their family members. They don't abandon their kids and run away

4.5 - *1 Samuel 17:17-18*

with another man or woman. Kingdom champions don't hold eternal grudges with their siblings. They seek family peace and progress and they pursue it with all of their strength.

Community Service
Kingdom champions are men and women who want to see good happen to others simply because they are humans and God's creation too. They want to see the earth filled with the glory of the knowledge of God as the water covers the sea. The best part of your resume for rising may not necessarily be your lofty education or your last well paid employment. On the contrary the best preparation for the top in your resume may be the unwritten good deed you undertook just for the sake of mankind at one level or the other. We live in a generation obsessed with reward in finance, fame and other fortunes; a generation where serving even in the Church must come with some lucre. Champions do it because someone has to do it. They see a cause for it to be done **[4.6]**. David asked a rhetoric from his opposing brother when they were wondering why he would take such a big risk even though he wasn't on the army's payroll as of then. All that a kingdom champion needs to get the job done is just a 'just cause'; not necessarily a personal cause, not a fame seeking cause. A communal cause is enough for them to be triggered into action. Kingdom champions won't fold their hands while others are suffering just because their own sheep are well kept. They see the need for a greater cause and give it a pursuit.

4.6 - *1 Samuel 17:28-29*

In like manner, kingdom champions won't win at the expense of the kingdom. Believers need to give priority to causes greater than their own little interpretation of a verse of the bible or their idol of doctrine. Many won't mind tearing apart and pulling down the whole Church and what the body Christ stands for just to fight some personal petty fights and personal interpretation of a scripture. They will rather ridicule the blessing of God in the lives of His people just to argue a doctrinal point against prosperity and the preachers thereof. They will rather discredit healing and miracles or whatever supernatural acts God sent to comfort His people to make unbelievers happy and be called true prophets. Kingdom race is a personal race and a communal race at the same time. Jesus, writing to the seven churches in Asia in the book of Revelation laid little emphasis on individual achievements and faults but rather addressed the Church in the spirit of community [4.7].

Kingdom champions are mindful of the community of saints and will never hurt it. They won't collect money from church members who trusted them because they are brethren and run away without fulfilling their obligation(s) as agreed before money was given.

Kingdom champions won't go about sowing evil seeds of discord among brethren to win friends and look better in the eyes of men. Kingdom champions don't go about snatching the spouses of Church members because God is forgiving. Kingdom Champions don't go about hurting sisters in the Church, sowing wild oats around and

4.7 - Revelation Chapters 2&3

leaving ladies like half-eaten chicken on the plate of hurt and frustrations because they are out to please their own urges. Kingdom champions think deeply of the effect of their actions on the community of saints before misbehaving. The worst rebuke David had from God came when he, against his own character, gave the unbeliever opportunity to blaspheme the name of the Lord and thus the Kingdom community **[4.8]**.

Costly Service
True services are costly, and kingdom champions are just ready to pay the price. Jesus paid His own price and simply said if anyone is not ready to pay the price, such is not fit for the championship of the kingdom. Even God paid the price with the blood of His own son to redeem us. He stooped low and took a position of weakness and temporarily losing to the kingdom of darkness with the fall of the first Adam and later the death of Christ. But once the temple was pulled down finally, the champion said "it is finished" on the cross. Part of what was finished was the payment for redemption of God's best and foremost creation, even mankind.

Serving will cost time if any champion will evolve in his or her true colour. It takes the sacrifice of time to train in and fine tune the art of winning. What you can't give the best of your time to can't give the best of the crown to you. David rose up very early to run the errand that brought him to lime light **[4.9]**. Whatever can't take the best from you won't deliver the best to you. Jesus said we should seek the kingdom of God "first", and the word first there

4.8 - 2 Samuel 12:14; 4.9 - 1 Samuel 17:20

signifies the best of your time. No kingdom champion can be a part time kingdom seeker; they are full time kingdom seekers whereas every other pursuit then follow suit. Most people seeking "emergency fix and treatment" all over churches are never pasture seekers who are lying down by the side of still waters. They are passers-by who just want to be fixed so they can go back to their wandering. They only popped in to get a wife, husband, deliverance, some money, political appointments and so on. True champions in God's kingdom invest quality time into personal development the kingdom way. Seed and harvest are linked with time in this kingdom. Ceaseless harvest requires ceaseless seed time.

Kingdom service for kingdom champions also cost material investments. David kept dedicating the material gold and silver he brought from battle fronts to God and the victory did not cease [4.10]. Even the sword of Goliath that weighed so much in shekels of gold and could have gone viral for sales online was placed in the temple by David as part of the champion's kingdom investment. I have seen people stop giving in Church because they have issue with prosperity matter, and yet they still go to such Church and enjoy the amenities therein. Firstly, our giving is unto the Lord, no matter how unfaithful the priests may be. Jesus knew Judas was stealing and yet money was being given into the ministry purse. Judas' day of judgement eventually came anyway. When Eli's children were messing around with the giving of God's people, God didn't command His people to stop

4.10 - 2 Samuel 8:10-11

bringing offerings to His house; He simply judged the priests when their cups were full. I will never let anyone rob me of my crown with his or her own unfaithfulness. Giving to the Church of Christ is giving to Christ, the high priest of the Church, in the order of Melchisedec. Many uncalled saints have simply started Churches because their tithe and giving is too big to be given to another Church while they remain an "ordinary deacon or member", as far as they are concerned. God wants us to serve Him with our substance, not to lobby for positions in the church or to attract attention for a return. Kingdom champions are simply addicted and all addictions carry costs depending on the value of the substance therein.

Gifted but Given

One of the dangers of being gifted is the tendency to overlook the fact that you were given the gift. Whether a natural gift like singing, speaking, administration or supernatural gifts in any shape or form; a man can receive nothing except he be given from above. David knew without ambiguity that he was given the skills he possessed. He spoke of how God trained his hands to war and his fingers to battle so that he could break a bow of steel with his hands.

The second side to gifting is to know that not only were you given your gift but you are now given as a gift to mankind by the reason of your gifting. No one is gifted in this kingdom for personal accolades and aggrandisements. Using the fivefold ministry as an epitome of divine call unto championship in life, we were told that it was a high call. Indeed a high call that turned gifted men and women unto gifts themselves; gifts of purpose given to the body of Christ for edification and to humanity as light [4.11]. Kingdom champions are gifts of purpose endowed to their generations so that they can spend and be spent for the kingdom of their king. No anointed vessel is bigger than the service for which he or she is anointed for. Don't ever take your eye off the service for which you were called and gifted for. Don't take your eye off God, his kingdom and his saints; for this cause you were sent and unto this purpose you were called.

You are a serving champion.

4.11 - Ephesians 4:7-12

Chapter Five

CHAMPION OF FAITH AND WISDOM

Kingdom champions are dealing not only with flesh and blood, but also with kingdoms of spirits and thus need more than strong will and mental prowess to emerge as the true champions which they are. Faith is more than strong head and stubbornness for the champion. Faith is not just having a will of steel; faith is the bridge between champions and the world of the unseen from where they draw virtues.

Faith Towards God

There is a place for healthy self-esteem and believing in one's self in the race and battles of life for champions. But faith is beyond self-belief and good self-esteem. Goliath was one man with huge self-esteem and self-belief, but it never translated to moving mountains for him. Rather than moving mountains, it was Goliath that got moved and destroyed. It takes more than being motivated in the kingdom of God to walk in the victorious procession of faith.

Faith, for kingdom champions, is the response of the spirit in positive affirmation towards God on whatever He had promised to do or confirm to have done. Champions take God for who He says He is and relate with Him as such. "The Lord is my shepherd", said David to God's promise of guidance, protection and provision; even though taking the position of a sheep sounds derogatory for humans.

Faith towards God is to believe that God does exist as who He said He is according to His word, and to believe that He rewards or responds to whoever reaches out to Him the right way **[5.1]**. God is not a title or a name of one of the supreme beings, but the description for the self-existing and most supreme uncreated one. God is not a Jew nor is he white or black; God is described with human terms for clarity only, but God is not a man. The beginning of grasping the concept of the Godhead is to divorce one's mind from what religion and contemporary wisdom paint Him to be. The beginning of faith is to know that God is what the word calls Him all over the Bible and relate with Him as such.

God was not voted in by the United Nations, neither was he endorsed by the G8 to be God. He needs not the approval of the American President or senate neither does He need image laundering of the western press to be God. Atheists have come and gone but God still remains the same. Because God is not petty enough to be jumping down to fight human rebellion now and then doesn't compromise His eternal existence and control over the universe. God is long suffering and will still judge the living and the dead one day when He chooses to do so. In the interim, the duty of the living is to believe that God is who He says He is. This is the foundation of faith in God.

5.1 - *Hebrews 11:6*

God Is
David didn't see God and I doubt he felt God, but he knew he had a shepherd in God; or how else could he have slain a lion and a bear without getting maimed. Kingdom champions lay all trophies at the feet of God even though they did their own human best to get the victories. This is acknowledging the existence of God, not merely as omnipresent one of the universe but as the very present help in your own life. To acknowledge the presence of God in your own life is part of faith towards God **[5.2]**. David said *"God was in my life when I killed the lion and the bear and the same God is in my life as I face this giant called Goliath today"*. Champions don't go it alone, they go with God. Kingdom Champions have no point to prove beyond affirming the supremacy of their king; his presence, power and glory. Champions don't think it's their money that gets the job done even though they spent some money on the project. Champions don't think it's their skills, connections or natural endowments that gets the job done. Champions know that except the Lord builds the house, they labour in vain that build it. Kingdom champions know that God is the one who gets the job done.

God Rewards
God rewards faith; He rewards believing His promises and so acting in accordance to the terms therein. For example, when fear, cares and anxiety come calling in your heart; the word of promise is to have no place for them but to make your request known to God in prayers

5.2 - *1 Samuel 17:37*

and thanksgiving **[5.3]**. Doing these guarantee the garrison of peace to be built round your innermost being whereby nothing shall eventually be missing which you need nor anything broken to damage or hurt you. Champions act out their faith based on God's promises; they don't just believe the believing, they do the doing. David honoured God with praise and worship in dancing without fear of being taken for a fool when the Ark of God was brought back to Jerusalem; God in return honoured him till death as the most celebrated king of Israel. The national flag of the natural nation of Israel today is the Star of David. Jesus and we His saints are sitting together on the right hand side of majesty today on the very throne of David **[5.4]**.

God rewards the trusts of His people on His faithfulness. Champions trust God's integrity and so judge Him faithful never to fail to show up at the right time in a right way. On many occasions when he would have taken the law into his own hand in haste, David left his case with Saul at the supreme court of heaven for God the righteous and faithful one to judge, and surely, God judged the case faithfully on the side of him who trusted God. Champions leave whatever they have given to God with God and know that He is faithful to keep it till the day of Christ. The reason why many will rather take short cuts having waited for a while for the Lord to show up is because their faith in God's faithfulness to show up at the right time is compromised. God will never wait a second beyond the set time. Faith towards God trusts divine clock for the appointed time.

5.3 - Philippians 4:6-7; *5.4* - Isaiah 9:7

God also rewards the persuasion of His champion in His ability to deliver; this also is faith towards God. It takes a champion who was fully persuaded in the ability of God as a man of war for a seventeen year old to be running towards Goliath, a veteran of repute with a sling and five stones. Mind you, Goliath had an amour bearer and wore a helmet over his head. The space left for target would have been so small that only God's eagle eyes could take it at one attempt without missing. We were not told that David had a telescope to guide the sling; all he had was persuasion in the able eye of the Lord which runs to and fro the whole earth and thus could not have missed a space for load delivery on the forehead of a man fighting his army. With experience of divine dealings, champions know that if God could kill a lion and a bear He could kill a Goliath as well. If He can kill sin, He can kill sicknesses and diseases; He can kill poverty, depression and all the attacks of the enemy in one shot. Champions know that if God could keep them so far, He is also able to keep them even further till the end. It is of the Lord's mercy that champions are not consumed by the race and battles of life. His compassions fail not but are new every morning, and great is his faithfulness.

Faith for Supernatural Help
Champions are not self-made; champions are helped to win again and again. God helps and compels help for His kingdom champions till the ever conquering one in them is fully at work. Someone brought David's application to fight Goliath forward to Saul, even though he didn't have

a direct access to the king as of then. Jonathan helped David severally even against his own interest in Saul's court. When David would have been killed by Saul's assassins one night, Saul's daughter helped him to escape with a disguise at the expense of her dad's interest. The priest of God couldn't withhold even the hallowed bread from David if only to receive strength from fainting. He gave him the sword of Goliath kept in the Temple museum for a memorial, and all was done at the expense of his entire family and fellow priests. People came out to help David in the bush he ran to; people helped him till he was enthroned as promised by God. In all of these, the mind-set of David was simply captured in this sweet psalm – *"when I remember you upon my bed and meditate on you in the night watches. Because you have been my help, therefore in the shadow of your wings I will rejoice. My soul follows close behind you; your right hand upholds me"* **[5.5]**.

Kingdom champions know that they can't do it alone, so they look up to God to send help. They know that once God helps, every help needed would show up. No one is an island is the true saying, but champions allow God to orchestrate their helps lest they go into idolatry while seeking human help. True help from God are like angels; they take the back stage in your life while helping you and still allow your God to be the centre of worship. Once a helper starts demanding to sit upon the stars of heaven in your life as a condition, you might be dealing with Lucifer in flesh without knowing. Turn away from such and turn to God.

Faith towards God takes your eyes off the help itself,

5.5 - *Psalm 63:6-8*

whichever form it comes; faith in God sets your eyes on the helper, even God of heavens and the earth.

Faith against Mountains
Goliath was a mountain of sort in flesh, but he came down crashing in the presence of a mountain moving champion called David. Champions don't wish the mountains don't exist; neither do they sit down fantasising that the mountain is smaller. Champions simply move the mountains. Kingdom champions are faith champions, mountain moving faith is their familiar territory. They beat down mountains and hill small with the sword of their mouth and allow the wind of the spirit to blow same away. If thou shall say to this mountain be thou removed and cast to the yonder and won't doubt, it shall be done, said Jesus to his company of champions **[5.6]**. David wouldn't keep quiet for once for Goliath because the mountain moving faith in him had no mute button on its remote. As Goliath was raging, so was David the champion talking. What of if it doesn't work out that way the sceptics around would have been saying? It made no difference to kingdom champion. Faith that moves mountains has no "what of if" behind it. The absence of "what if it doesn't work out well" behind the declarations of the champion is what makes it mountain moving word of faith. It is not yet faith, if in your heart there is a possibility for failure. Take your time and work on the faith substance before setting out moving mountains. Deal with the doubts and fears of failure first if you sense they are still there; don't just assume victory, get victory as a tangible substance in the presence of God before setting out addressing mountains.

5.6 - Mark 11:23-24

It is not uncommon for our hearts to be overwhelmed within us when we are faced with daunting mountains of life. The fact that your heart still gets overwhelmed on the matter shows that the relativity of height is not yet in your favour as it were. A mountain whose ends you can't see while it's still standing is one you might not be able to move to yonder. You need to see beyond the mountain into the yonder where it could be moved into before you start laying demand on the movement into the yonder. What you therefore need is not an extra eye but extra height in God. You see, God is the highest that is and will ever be. When you are overwhelmed by life, go all the way after the highest God. Create qualitative time in seeking His face especially in the word and prayers with thanksgiving, and He will soon take you to a rock that is higher than you. There you will see the end of the mountain and even the yonder it could be cast into. When you come down to face the mountain, your top of the rock view will give you the confidence to say "move" to the mountain and never doubt again. You can never move a mountain you are not higher than; all champions need a rock that is higher than them for faith height. David knew this so well and he said he would cry to God in prayers when his heart was overwhelmed [5.7]. True faith prays, God is a rewarder of them that diligently seek him. Talk is cheap, faith is not cheap talk, and faith is hard work. Hard work in word, hard work in obedience and hard work in prayer, hard work in renewal of strength. Mountains of trouble will move when you address it from the "top of the mountain view" of possibility.

5.7 - *Psalm 61:1-3*

Supernatural Know-how

Kingdom champions are skilled in the art of conquering and maintaining the integrity of their victory, simply because God himself is skilled at same. God by wisdom made the heaven and the earth, not just by power. Kingdom champions are not the smartest as such but they borrow from higher wisdom. David didn't just ask to be shown the rock that was higher than him so that he would climb by himself. He pleaded to be led there in... *"lead me to a rock that is higher than I".*

It is not enough to plead for open doors from heaven, it is also important to ask for wisdom of navigating same. David was thrown into limelight after killing Goliath and what looked like an invitation to enjoy in the king's palace came as the beginning of his journey into the dangerous terrain of power politics. It may take power to win; it will take wisdom to last and enjoy the fruits of conquest. Power and might will help you win and be crowned a champion, but reigning after your coronation is achieved strictly by wisdom **[5.8]**. One can use feminine or masculine power to win a relationship and marriage but building a goodly and peaceable home requires loads of wisdom. Prayers can position you for a job but it takes more than prayers to deliver on the job and secure upward movement.

David soon realised that winning Goliath of Gath in the valley of Elah was a child's play compared to winning the invisible battle of attrition in the palace of Saul. The battle extended all over the terrains of Israel, involving every skill and wit David could muster to stay alive **[5.9]**.

5.8 - Proverbs 8:15; 5.9 - 1 Samuel 18:7-16

Relating Aright

Being a champion means you are unique and divinely endowed with the ability and capacity to be a blessing not only to yourself and your immediate family members, but to a wider range of humanity. This necessitates God to raise you among a wide range of people as well. Some good and wonderful while some will be like thorns in the flesh at times. Even if your upbringing is strictly nuclear and fenced, you still can't afford to be parochial when it comes to relating with people especially outside your immediate family circle. God in the course of preparing you to maximize the greater one in you will expose you to all kinds of human beings, so that you can develop the wits of dealing with all without losing your ornament of grace and fragrance of life. No one can be a true champion by isolation; you need to relate with people of diverse personalities to be truly blessed and be a blessing. Every champion needs wisdom of dealing with four categories of people that will be brought their way in the cause of their journey:

(i). Dealing with Authority in Wisdom – It is of great interest in the kingdom of God that authorities are paramount and not joked with. Order and tranquillity is in heaven because authority is in place and any breach of same could not be tolerated but flushed out. Anarchy is of the kingdom of this world, even the kingdom of darkness. Whatever promotes anarchy, disorderliness and lack of submission to the rightly constituted authority will open doors for the adversary in a matter of time, no matter how justifiable it seems in the first instance. There is a way to

press home your points and deal with abuse of authority without you creating a state of anarchy. It is called the way of wisdom and it will end up in your enthronement rather than destruction as a rebel.

There are three level of authorities recognised by God and must be preserved as much as possible. **Parental authority, Civil authority and Spiritual authority** are set along our ways from birth till death to keep us on the narrow path that leads to life and keep us from the broadways of defeat, failure and perdition. David recognised these three levels of authorities and he didn't breach his journey into greatness by breaching any of those. David was that young man who submitted himself to his parental guidance even after he was anointed to be king over Israel by the prophet of the Lord. He was looking after the family sheep even after oil had been poured on him. He was sent on errand by his father to go and deliver food for his brothers in battle front even though he had just been anointed to be king over all of them a few months earlier. At a stage in David's career as an army officer, he was demoted from the brigade of guard to become a captain of a thousand by the king who was envious and afraid of his fame, but he still went about his new assignment in wisdom **[5.10]**. As a result of acting in wisdom, his dominion over the evil spirit controlling Saul was not compromised. Saul was afraid of him the account said. Divine presence with him was real and the people loved him with favour as a result. Not acting in wisdom can shut the door of favour God is opening and diminish the believer's aura of dominion.

5.10 - *1 Samuel 18:13-16*

David didn't lead a mutiny or stage a coup against the leader as a result; even though he knew he was being monitored and put in uncomfortable positions. He wasn't busy throwing tantrum and fouling up the atmosphere with moods and attitudes. At times, you can be more noticeable or gifted in a setting and thus attract envy especially from people high up or even your contemporaries; this is not the time to start throwing tantrum around and be fighting against the envy in flesh like a commoner. Champions don't fight like street urchins. Be gracious even in the face of envy and back stabbing. Don't lower your status to that of your adversary. Dealing with anyone in authority can be tricky and dangerous, and you need to be wise. Many have been denied opportunities of expressions simply because they were not wise enough in dealing with the authority. Civil authority ranges from government officials, law enforcement officers, teachers, coaches and superiors in work places. While they are in that position, they carry a measure of power which can make or mar destinies. Relate with them in wisdom and rise up to shine as a star which you are **[5.11]**.

While running away from Saul, he came to a place called Nob where a man by the name Ahimelech was God's priest and represented the spiritual authority on David as of that material time. Ahimelech demanded sexual purity from David and his men before they could eat the hallowed bread which was available in the temple. David didn't call a bluff of him and call him old school, he duly observed the motion before an anointed and God kept

5.11 - *Proverbs 16:14-16*

him alive. Saul on the other hand killed the same priest but the respective ends of David and Saul said it all about who acted in wisdom. It is not weakness to deal with authority in wisdom; it is safety and strength.

(ii). Dealing with Helpers in wisdom – All along your journey into greatness, God will place certain people along your way as helpers or ladders to climb through. They will most likely and even surely not be perfect just as you are not. They may have their own vested interest for helping you as well; they may be annoying at times. Nevertheless, if they are sent helpers from God, then they are needful at this phase of your life. Keep and relate well with them in spite of their short comings. David understood this concept with wisdom so much that he dealt with the dysfunctional attitudes among his men of war without jeopardising the ranks and cause.

A man by the name Joab and his two brothers were among the men who had been with David from the onset; very loyal to David but volatile in attitude. It was he and his brother that David lamented over many times on how to deal with, knowing fully well they were sent to help him establish his kingdom. He described them in one of his psalms as prickly thorns who could only be handled by a man wearing a coat of iron. Fighting Joab will send a wrong signal to the rank and file of a vulnerable kingdom. The fact that someone was sent by God to help you doesn't mean they can't be borrowed of the devil. Saul was a thorn in David's flesh, but it was the same Saul that gave David his first chance of breakthrough in life.

You might not even like some helpers sent your way by God but if they are needed for your establishment, they will have to be tolerated. Your character as a champion will be refined further as you do so. Wisdom is your coat of iron to handle men and women who prove to be thorns and yet carry the rose you need on them.

(iii). Dealing With Followers In Wisdom – People gravitate towards success naturally; if you are wining, you will have followers in one form or the other. Ranging from children at home, to junior colleagues at work, audience in congregations, clients for your goods and services, mentees and followers in any other form. Your wisdom is to first deal with your followers with empathy as one sent to look after their interests above even yours.

Followership is based on trust, irrespective of how good what you have to offer is. Followers must be sure their good interest is your goal. On one occasion, in the cause of pursuing a band of raiders that attacked David's company at a place called Ziklag, some of his men got so tired they could not follow on in the pursuit and eventual battle. On returning from the battle with success story, David insisted they must be given part of the goods and glory as well. It further established his leadership as not a mere user and glory hunter but a leader with a heart **[5.12]**. Comparing such wisdom with the folly of one of David's grandson by the name Rehoboam, the son of Solomon, he cared not about the feelings and hurts of his followers and soon lost his kingdom **[5.13]**. It is wisdom to

---

5.12 - 1 Samuel 30:21-25; *5.13* - 1 Kings 12:1-24

be fair with your followers. Oppression is folly and must not be found among kingdom champions.

(iv). Dealing with Adversaries in Wisdom – The job of an adversary is to distract a champion from his or her path of pursuit. It takes wisdom to deal with adversaries. Some you will need to confront and some you will need to ignore. Even doing either of the above also has its own right time for it to be right. When Absalom rebelled and overthrew David in a palace coup, a man by the name Shimei was there on the way mocking David. There was enough on the plate of the champion then than executing revenge then or even when he was restored. He left the judgement of Shimei to another generation. Adversaries are going nowhere; you are the one running a race and fighting bouts of the championship. Your job is to make sure you don't abandon your primary pursuit and join them on the way side of life.

Discretion and Judgement

Decision making is part of everyday life and very crucial for champions to have sound judgement and discretion rather than hasty impulsive attitude. Discretion is an offshoot of wisdom of God; it gives you the right judgment in the face of dilemma. Right judgement will empower your will to do right, right action will bear right results and generate the right emotion overall. You don't have to live your life in regrets for wrong decisions and steps taken in carelessness. Discretion is not a gift per say, it is an inner character you develop through observation with the eye of the spirit **[5.14]**. Kingdom champions are deep in

5.14 - *Proverbs 3:19-24*

the inside, they procure safety from within irrespective of the danger outside. Discretion and sound judgement without muddling life up with mere emotions is a character of wisdom; champions develop it with experience of wise observations.

Ideas for Victories

Finally, on this note on champion's wisdom, it is needful for us to know that faith will procure us victory but the delivery of same is by wisdom. Borrowing heaven's idea makes champions look smart on earth. Champions are not necessarily the smartest or the strongest but they trade on higher ideas. In natural warfare, intelligence plays a major role in success. So much resources and time are spent to gather and analyse enough intelligence report before making any engagement, as these will play major role in determining losing or winning eventually. The powerful nations in warfare today are not the most populous with the largest army, but the largest intelligence gatherers. So important is the art of gathering intelligence that satellites are planted in the heavenly spaces far above the earth for the same purpose. If natural men are reaching for higher eyes to see into their victory, so much more do you need to prioritize acquiring supernatural wisdom for winning ideas on earth. Champions can't afford to be clueless and shallow; the know-how to bring out the good in you into the place of profitability is wisdom. Develop your know-how; don't stagnate in ignorance, kingdom champions don't get stranded in the race and battle of life. When you know the right thing to do, your fidgeting disappears and you exhume confidence even when the results seem not coming in as fast as you envisaged. Wisdom makes for boldness and boldness makes for victory **[5.15]**. You can't be an ambassador of a great nation and be timid. Timidity in the face of challenges is a reflection that wisdom for what to do is lacking.

Henceforth, you shall radiate the confidence and glory of the kingdom of God which you represent, with all boldness and confidence rooted in wisdom.

5.15 - *Ecclesiastes 8:1*

Chapter Six

BAKED IN FURNACE

Every gold material in the ore that escaped the refiner's fire yesterday is still lying somewhere as lump of earth till date. Laying there just like any other escapee with no beauty and of virtually no use. The tried and tested ones which have passed through the process of refining are the shinning pieces in the market place of life the whole world is dying to possess today. Every champion is made of precious material like gold; they need refining anyway. The story of becoming is never complete until the furnace takes it proper place in the process. No one is clapping and happy while going through the process of being refined for shinning. Shining is sweet and gratifying, so is refining is bitter but needful. Same way gold is refined for jewel so is clay well baked in furnace for fine pottery. The more the baking, the more glazed and beautiful the clay ware.

David was refined as gold and well baked as clay for the master's use. Resilience was built into him and shining placed on him in the furnace school of life. Even Joab his chief of army acknowledged the constant presence of furnace in David's upbringing in the school of destiny till his old age **[6.1]**. This statement was made when David was going through another furnace in the latter course of his reign. It is easy for an outsider to see the glitz and trophies of conquests champions carry and thus envy

6.1 - 2 Samuel 19:7

them, wanting to be them and even count them luckier in life. Far be it from being as cheap as it looks and sounds to be a champion. True champions may not lay emphasis on what they have gone through to arrive at a given port of glory, but be sure that the sail was rough and treacherous but for sufficient grace of heaven.

There are two kinds of furnaces of life every champion will come across; they are not the same, neither are they substitutes for each other. While one is out to refine you for your shining, the other is out to destroy you so that you don't shine. One is godly to do you good in your latter end, while the other is evil to hurt you, afflict you and prevent you from getting to your latter end. God allows us to be tried for our promotion and eventual glory but Satan's trial is not really a trial in the real sense but a scheme to destroy us. We say yes Lord to the school of heaven's trial while we resist the devil and its kingdom of darkness.

Refiner's Fire

God is likened to a refiner whose job is to bring the best out of His people so that they can fulfil their glorious destinies **[6.2]**. The job of a refiner is neither to pamper nor destroy the gold, but to extract it from dust and extract dust from it. Every champion is taken into God's school of shinning not as finished product but as a raw material with capacity to do well eventually. Some champions won't even know they are one initially until God starts allowing them to pass through the refining furnaces.

6.2 - *Malachi 3:1-4*

Then the greater one in them will start showing up with strong intensity and resilience they themselves never knew was there all along.

The first thing God's fire does is to take away the dross from our gold. Many baggage we carry along in life are nothing but weights besetting our smooth running. Every wise and experienced miner knows that not all that is scooped in a gold mine is gold, and not all is of value. The truth is that the gold in the mine is so little that a mountain of mined ore might not yield more than a small piece in metal eventually. But the value of the little refined piece in no small measure surpasses equivalent weight of dirt it was taken from. Where God is taking you is of more value and glory than what he is taking away from you in the process. Stop crying, champion, when God allows some loads to be taken off you. As valuable as the loss seems, it is of far lesser value to what your eventual shining is worth to the kingdom. Stop counting your loss, if God took them or allow them taken. They are worth less than the value you placed on them. Every refiner knows gold when he/she sees one; God knows what it is worth, agree with him and be free from junk as soon as possible.

The second reason God allows you to pass through furnaces on your way to glory is to build strength and resilience in you eventually. Gold ore is a lump of earth that crumbles on application of pressure but pure gold has better tensile and compressive capacities once it comes out refined. The level of impurity or non-gold material remaining in a gold piece determines its value in carats. The higher the carats, the better and less fading the gold; the stronger is the gold's staying power in the face of wear and tear. Your eventual staying power in life is a function of how much strength you have imbibed along the way. Furnace is a place of imbibing strength, stop crying for branching therein. It is not the final destination but a mere stop over for strength acquisition. God doesn't want the strength of your prosperity to be built on mere availability of money, so He allowed you to pass through a period of scarce money supply to imbibe strength over financial worries. The scarcity of human support at the onset of that project in your hand is not a death sentence on the project. It is a mere furnace to imbibe the strength of looking up like David for divine, rather than looking around for human approval like Saul. Every champion going to a land of wealth flowing with milk and honey will learn to first imbibe the strength of character while feeding on mere manna. Every champion who will be preferred by God for the throne to the heir apparent will first be forsaken and over looked by men of his own household at the ordination service. Every cornerstone chosen by God eventually had gone through the furnace of rejection by the builder.

The third reason God allows us to go through furnace is to make our reliance on Him a total and enduring one. God is not so insecure that He craves our reliance on him so much for his own personal gratification as it were. God wants our total reliance because He knows we shall come across challenges that are beyond our capabilities on the path He had chosen for us. He therefore wants us to totally rely on Him so that when we come across what is beyond us we won't run back. For champions, the race of life must only be in one direction and it's a forward direction. There are giants on the way who will want to scare us as Goliath was to the army of Israel. It takes a man like David who had been left alone in the bush to look after the sheep in lion and bear infested forests to know what it is like to stand up and be counted. He stood up not in self-reliance or self-pity but in total reliance on God.

It is natural for champions to have a sense of self-reliance because of efforts they have put into self-development. It is easy for champions to be over-confident because it takes huge confidence to dare being a champion in the first place. It is easy for champions to suffer from bouts of ego that over rate their abilities because they have gotten the jobs done before and people around tell them how good they are. God allows us to pass through furnace of life to purge us of all such unhealthy "self-something and over-something-". In our place of crying for help when the going gets rough beyond our preparations, we find His grace as the only all sufficient strength we need. It is then we come out void of over-confidence, over-rating and self-reliance. God's fire is not out to mar us but to make us, the sooner we imbibe the lesson He is passing across, the quicker our refining process and the less time we spend therein. The children of Israel spent forty years in a class meant for forty days simply for being stubborn and stiff necked; a people not ready to dance to the divine tune.

When David said God had taught his hands to war and his fingers to battle so that a bow of iron he had broken with his hands, it simply shows what furnace the hands and fingers had gone through. Champions are not softies, their trainings are intense, time-tied and void of distractions.

Enemy's Fire

The fire of the enemy is kindled to burn, mar and destroy us; it is started to steal from champions all that they have piled up over the years **[6.3]**. It is therefore your responsibility to quench it and not endure or explain it away. **[6.4]**. God is good and there is no evil in Him at all. He doesn't try any man with evil, but same can't be said of the prince of this world. The furnace of the wicked is called the fiery darts of the devil. We are sent and meant to put it out by faith without fear or favour. Whatever fire you tolerate, you can't quench. Faith starts with total and absolute intolerance for evil. Kingdom champions don't sit on the fence when it comes to good and evil, light and darkness. Billions are spent all over the world by various secular bodies to fight sickness, diseases, hunger and poverty. If these are not evil, it would have been virtuous to spread and perpetuate them rather than fighting them. They are evil just like every other works of the devil meant to kill, steal and destroy what belong to us. It is ours to resist and our weapon of mass resistance is faith. I wrote extensively on the faith to quench the fiery

6.3 - John 10:10; *6.4* - Ephesians 6:10-16

darts or fire of the devil in one of my books titled *"EQUIPPED FOR VICTORY".*

Don't' Get Burnt
Just as God's fire is a school to refine, the enemy's fire is a school of affliction. It is not the wish of God for you to be burnt and destroyed. God's fire doesn't burn nor destroy His own children. In extreme cases when God allows the enemy's fire to burn his children, it must have been as result of perpetual refusal to yield to God's call away from such fire. Disobedience and stubbornness will expose a champion to affliction and God can't help till you turn away.

Peradventure you have been or you are being burnt right now; your turn-around starts now as you turn and learn what God is showing you. The enemy has no over-riding power over your precious life and destiny; it takes your allowance for him to get a foothold. Reject Satan's invitation to his school of affliction. Stay your ground in Christ and see what God is saying.

Champions easily get burnt in the enemy's fire kindled by disobedience, not by the fury of the wicked kindled because Satan is evil. The three Hebrew children will testify that no one can hurt you when you are a follower of that which is good indeed **[6.5]**. Instead of destruction, whichever furnace the enemy means for evil will always result in promotion for you henceforth.

Many are the afflictions of the righteous was the cry of

6.5 - *Daniel 3:1-30*

David the champion, but the Lord delivers him from them all he also testified **[6.6]**. God's deliverance is total and absolute from all evils and it's your turn now to testify.

6.6 - *Psalm 34:16-22*

Chapter Seven

CHAMPION IN LOVE

The subject of love draws universal attention and affection, but in no other kingdom is love given a status of law as in the kingdom of God. Love is optional and by choice in the kingdoms of men, people can pick and choose who to love and otherwise but not so in the kingdom of champions. In the kingdom of God, loving is living; love became the only law after Christ was given in love **[7.1]**.

The whole volume of commandments, laws and ordinances given to Moses by God due to the non-evolvement (hardness) of the hearts of people was replaced by just two laws once Christ brought the fullness of dispensation of God's kingdom here on earth. Love used to be reciprocal before Christ came, but on the advent of the Kingdom of God here on earth, love became a law with or without reciprocity. It is noble to love when one is sure of being loved back but for champions it is not the case. Love is a calling for the kingdom champions.

Loving God

David loved the Lord and it was not hidden. He took his life in his hand to face Goliath simply because Goliath was defiling **"the army of the Lord"**. The shame of the

7.1 - Mathew 22:35-40

Lord was David's shame. Since love is nebulous in nature, it can only be described by the effect it produces in actions and inactions. For champions, love is more than mere emotional expressions which fluctuate according to the happenings around us. Love is more than a mere sayings but a deep seated character within us with which we relate with God.

(i). *To love God is to be faithful to him*

David understood loyalty to God as the foundation to the concept of loving God. To love God is not to just sing Church songs with emotions even though loving God will make us sing His praise wholeheartedly and with emotions. To love God is beyond merely saying it; it is a call unto deep loyalty to God and His kingdom. To love God is to be on His side no matter what the situation is and who is there or not. The cause of God will be worth dying and living for once the love of God sets in. Champions develop the character of love towards God by firstly developing a loyal bond towards God from the inside. The loyalty we are talking of is also known as faithfulness. God doesn't need to be watching over you with a big stick to rein you in. You are given to Him and His kingdom and you have reached your last bus stop. Champions' allegiance to the king and His kingdom is not conditional, it has nothing to do with who else is there loving God or who is not. Doing what is popular because one will look odd and out of place if one doesn't do it is not the same as love. People have gotten married because others are doing so and they don't want to look odd; that is not the same as getting married because you are in love. For the former, loyalty and faithfulness can't be guaranteed. Same with the love of God. It's good to be brought up or live among people who love God and things of God and thus join them doing same. It is however better to develop a personal relationship with God and fall in love with Him personally. When the environment and circumstances change, the love will remain. In this age of towing the path of popular opinion and political correctness in order not to be given a bad name, champions need to know that they owe their allegiance to God first and to His kingdom. Champion allegiance to any denomination, race, nationality and any other cause no matter how noble, must be secondary. You are firstly loyal to God the king and His kingdom before your loyalty to your local assembly can make sense and be rewarded in the court of heaven. Anything done at the expense of the kingdom of God no matter how noble it sounds is disloyalty and not done out of love of God. It could be out of love for something else but not the love of God. Hear what David the champion admonished. ***"O love the Lord all ye his saints; for the Lord preserves the faithful"*[7.2]**.

(ii). To Love God is to Hate Evil

God and evil are word and opposite in every sense of it. When we love God, we can't love evil at the same time. To go to church or be a clergy does not guarantee the hatred of evil but to love God does. To hate evil doesn't mean not to be tempted with evil or even to fall in an extreme bad case, but it still means to hate it. When you hate evil, you will resist doing evil right from the thought processes; when we hate evil we won't do it. In case we then find

7.2 - Psalm 31:23a

ourselves to have done it, same hatred for it must not be compromised. With the same hatred, we must come out of it in repentance and take a new path. To love God means we can't be practising evil. If we commit that which is evil or we are struggling with same, we won't be giving excuses, but rather we will seek help. People who truly love God don't defend evil neither will they be joining nor forming groups to fight the word of God and His people in order to do that which is evil. (Selah). The love of God is not rooted in our sexual feelings like this generation wants us to believe it. Kingdom champions develop the character of love - the love of God which is to hate evil. Even though we are to love everyone including the ones doing evil, nevertheless, we must not love evil. We must not endorse evil in any form or shade. Kingdom champions can't love their political party manifestos if it contradicts the love of God. Political or economic gain must not come first for kingdom champions, the love of God must supersede any other interest in our hearts; the love of God is to hate evil. David the champion has this to say to us. ***"You who love the Lord hate evil, he preserves the soul of his saints, he delivers them out of the hand of the wicked"*** [7.3].

(iii). To Love God is to Appreciate Him
Our appreciations of God are in two folds; we appreciate Him simply for who He is and we appreciate Him for what He does. The beginning of character development in the love of God is to come to terms with His person. God is loving and gracious, merciful and kind, even though He is all powerful and holy. None of God's great attributes

7.3 - *Psalm 97: 10*

hinders Him from still being a good and loving father to His children. A God so holy and just would have been just tolerant of scheming and sliming ones which we were, but not in any sense. God loves us and thus tolerates us as He changes us to what He wants us to be no matter how slow we are in catching up. What the love of God demands from us is to love Him back with His love which He shed abroad in our heart. God therefore doesn't just stand afar and demanding love from us; He helps us to love Him back by the help of His Holy Spirit in us.

In like vein, we are to love God for His marvellous acts, His answers to our calls in prayer, the victory in the seen and unseen battles of life and all His good acts towards us. When David the champion saw God's attributes and acts in His life, he said it succinctly thus. **"I love the Lord because he has heard my voice and my supplications; because he has inclined his ear to me therefore I will call upon him as long as I live"** [7.4].

David wrote several songs of psalms in appreciation of God for who He is and what He did. He even wrote about what God will do out of love for God's person. He stood for what is good in the sight of God out of loyalty and faithfulness. Kingdom champions love God the king for who He is and what He is doing, they love Him by hating what He hates and love Him with all faithfulness and loyalty. This is what the love of God is. Loving God is beyond feelings but involves feelings; it is deep rooted allegiance that makes champions cleave to God with all

7.4 - Psalm 116:1-2

they are and have all their days.

Loving Mankind

It is absolutely impracticable to love God and not love mankind created in the image of God. Champions are human and are commanded to love humanity. No matter how much mountains we conquer and how much seas we navigate, if it is not to benefit mankind in love at long run, we have been stealing living and guilty of theft of existence. If God should come down and play the role by Himself, humanity won't be able to stand His awesome presence; that is why He sent us as ambassadors of love to do for mankind what He would have done. Kingdom champions are ambassadors of love; we are emissaries of divine kindness to the saints and sinners alike. David knew he was sent as an extension of God's kind of love to the people and thus he related with them as such.

(i).   To Love Mankind is to be Considerate

The golden rule of love is to do unto others as you would have them do unto you. It is easy to forget weakness and treat the weak as dung when we are in the position of strength. David's character of love was developed in this area so much that it didn't take Nathan much ado to convict him of his sin when he had Uriah's wife. The parable was simply of an inconsiderate rich man who would do to other man what he wouldn't have wanted done to him. Because it was out of character for David to be inconsiderate, he quickly felt guilty like a fish out of water [7.5]. The reason why people don't feel guilty about wrong doing is probably because the wrong doing is not out of character for them. Once it is not in your character to do so and you did, all you need is a little light and you will be convicted and make a turn never to do it again. It is in the character of champions to be considerate of others; they don't go about cheating others and taking that which is not theirs with impunity. They will treat others the same way they want to be treated. I have heard people talk of David like a habitual sinner! No, not in any way. Aside the case of Uriah the Hittite's wife, Beersheba the mother of Solomon, in no other account of the bible was it said that David committed such atrocity. He called it sin and repented before the Lord. He must have really felt bad for the woman as well and I believe that was why he promised her that Solomon shall be king. God was able to make a sense out of David's mess because he repented and turned. Same way he would do for any champion who falls and stands up in repentance to continue the journey of everlasting conquests.

Consider the way David treated Saul in backsliding. It was a considerate way of treating people in love. He didn't trample on Saul because Saul was in the position of weakness at that material time. Many soldiers of self-righteousness know how to trample on an already defeated kingdom warrior to win cheap popularity as being upright. If David had taken advantage of Saul's weak position, Absalom too would have succeeded in doing same to him when he was in a weak position later in life. Both David and Saul found themselves in such weak positions simply because they both sinned against

7.5 - *2 Samuel 12:1-3*

and came under the judgement of God. The results could have been the same but for the seed of love David had sown ahead of his destiny more than three decades before then. Kingdom champions must learn to walk in the middle of the road of standing for justice and uprightness without deviating to compromise on one side or judgemental trampling of the weak and fallen on the other side.

On another occasion when David's men were pursuing the Amalekite bandits who looted and plundered their camp in Ziklag, some of David's men were too tired to follow on in pursuit and fighting. He treated them well nevertheless not minding that they ought to be men of war and thus be resilient. He was considerate to those men in their days of weakness in the battle and it became an ordinance in Israel. Several decades later, David's day of weakness in battle too came and he was almost killed by a Philistine. As soon as this happened, the whole leadership willingly and unanimously excused his weakness and told him to stay behind from battle thenceforth. Nevertheless, the glories of the victories were not less his compared to when he was an active and agile fighter **[7.6]**. No member of the military rank saw the weakness in once a lion killer as the platform to plan coup and take over the throne. He had sown the love seed of treating others as he would be treated ahead in strength and then he reaped it in weakness.

(ii).   To Love Mankind is to Give People their Places
No champion is an island. God brings people across our way to midwife us into our greatness and even to keep us

7.6 - *2 Samuel 21:15-17*

in the greatness. It's not enough to know how much we need God-sent people while we are rising, we should also do so even in our risen position. The womb that carried the vulnerable foetus for nine months is relevant even after birth. Some will be brought across your way as a ladder to climb through while others are as supporting platforms when you get up there. In love, a champion must give people their places in the roll of honour. Show love by honouring people who are placed along your path by heaven for the purpose of your enthronement. In the kingdom, there is no luck or happenstance; the steps of the righteous are ordered by God. David remembered the role and place of Jonathan in his evolvement as a king and would't rest until he gave him and Saul the honour of decent burial in their own sepulchres, something crucial to the Jewish culture of their own day. No one is self-made in the real sense of it and to think otherwise is to be drowned in the pond of arrogance. David realised the place of Jonathan and knew that the best thing was to bring Jonathan's surviving son to the palace where he originally belonged. Destinies are personal but also inter-woven especially in this kingdom of champions. Except when people want to take the place of God in your life, don't hesitate to give people the honour they deserve. There is a honour for people ahead of you just as there is another honour for your contemporaries. There is also in like manner honour for your subordinates. No kingdom champion is allowed to be condescending and look down on people under them. God is high above all and yet He doesn't hesitate to call us kings, priests, lights and all the wonderful status He conferred on us. Making people feel inferior and lower than you to flex your might is not in the character of champions.

(iii) To Love Mankind is to Feel their Pains

Empathy is a great virtue for him that will gather people together in reigning. Strength without compassion breeds brute. The only reason God comforts us is for us to be able to comfort others with same comfort with which we are being comforted of him. It is needful for champions to know that pain is universal and others feel it as we do too. Same way you want succour in pain, you should succour others who are in same. It wasn't difficult for David to identify with folks in distress, pain, indebtedness and discontent while he was in the wilderness **[7.7]**. He never felt those ones deserved the pain for whatever reason while he was suffering unjustly in his own eye. It is easy to be tempted into thinking others deserve the trouble they are going through while we are just victims of wickedness who deserve better. No one deserves pain without relief. Champions are God's channel of relief to the oppressed and light to them who are in darkness. Our helping people must be solely to relieve them of pain and not to win accolades as being charitable or powerful. Jesus healed out of compassion, not because he wanted to be called powerful or to manipulate the healed into submission.

(iv). To Love Mankind is to Appreciate their Sacrifice

People will go out of their way to help you. God will put you in their hearts as a cause that must be accomplished and thus you must not take their sacrifices for granted. On one occasion, David was in the hold and wanted a

7.7 - *1 Samuel 22: 1-2*

show of bravery from his men because that was the only way they could take back Bethlehem from the host of the Philistines. All he needed to do was a simple lamentation that he could be given the water from the well in Bethlehem. His men, on hearing their leader's desire, took all the risks and broke through the host of Philistine to get the water and thus decimate the host of Philistines. When the water was given to David, he refused to gratify himself with it but poured it unto the Lord **[7.8]**. We need to humbly appreciate the sacrifices people make on our behalf for us to be where we are. Parental sacrifice, partner's sacrifice, leaders' and followers' sacrifices. It is needful to be humble enough and acknowledge the things people give up to help us rise up. In love, we need to show appreciation. Kingdom champions don't use people as instruments of gratification. They don't go around like Lucifer looking for who to use. They appreciate the sacrifice of others and thus stay humble before the Lord.

(v). To love Mankind is to See others' Efforts in the whole Picture
One man's success is a product of the collective efforts of many. Truly it's you that the trophy and crown would be given to but you need to see the efforts others had put in. The fact that you pay people to do what they are doing doesn't mean that they don't deserve appreciation. You should not just appreciate people to patronise them into servitude, you must appreciate them because they deserve appreciation as humans serving other humans. To watch after another man's vineyard is not quantifiable in monetary wage. When people therefore

7.8 - *2 Samuel 23:14-17*

are sent by God to watch over your vineyard, don't take it for granted. Kingdom champions are not allowed a sense of entitlement. To take people's kindness for granted because they are our spouse is entitlement and it destroys relationships. Same way in any other relationship; sense of entitlement destroys morale. The good you feel you are entitled to could have been taken from you and given to your neighbour who is better than you. Kingdom champions won't cheat people of their wage or rescind on an agreement at the detriment of others who had done their own part. Kingdom champions won't rob others of what is due to them in order to satisfy their own inordinate cravings.

On a final note, it takes the fear of God to love God and love mankind; every kingdom champion needs to develop a character of fear of the Lord. Fear of the Lord is to hold Him in awe and high esteem; it is to hold His word and His opinions as sacrosanct. Relating with an unseen God will then be like He is right there physically; relating with people also will be like God is watching. Hear this advice from David the champion:

"The spirit of the Lord spoke by me and his word was on my tongue, the God of Israel spoke to me. He who rules over men must be just ruling in the fear of God. And he shall be like light of the morning without clouds, like tender grass springing out of the earth by clear shining after rain" [7.9].

7.9 - *2 Samuel 23:2-4*

Chapter Eight

HUNTED BUT WINNING

Every champion is a treasure carrier, always hunted by the robbers of destiny. The enemy will do everything possible to destroy but once he knows he can't defeat a champion, the only option left is to distract same. Most champions who were brought down weren't destroyed by the might of the enemy but were played into self-destruction. The only time the devil was likened to a lion is in the hunting sense. The kingdom of darkness hunts for precious souls; anything available will be thrown at you as hunting weapon. The good news is that champions are configured for winning again and again **[8.1]**. Here, we see the testimony of David as a champion who had been hunted since his youth and yet was not prevailed over.

Hunted by Memories

One of Satan's biggest weapons of hunting is memory, just as he does with any other good thing through perversions. Memory can be perverted at the expense of the owner and to the advantage of the hunter. When a roe sees a lion, what comes to mind first is the memory of what it has seen done to its specie by the hunting specie over time and so a paralysing fear grips the hunted even before the chase begins. The pasts that hold people tight

8.1 - Psalm 129:1-2

at times are not even part of their makings; it could be a background they met on ground which the enemy tries hard to convert to their own foreground now. David was obviously a lone child of Jesse from a woman he most likely wasn't married to. When kings were considered, it quickly became convenient to hide the product of family scion's mis-behaviour at the backside of the farm to avoid embarrassment before the Lord and his anointed. Even after David was made, once he had a serious challenge in same area that bothers on having a child outside the wedlock, he was quickly reminded of his past by the hunter of destinies.

Condemnation for sins is not what heals but rather a change of way called repentance, and obtaining of mercy in forgiveness. The weight of condemnation stirred up the memory of David and soon he saw the flaw in character as a hereditary problem **[8.2]**. David didn't say all human were born in sin but himself. Maybe others have used such phrase to taunt him while he was growing up. They probably had said that the fault was his mum's. All of a sudden David himself began to queue up for a life time of guilt and condemnation. It is easy for people to believe they have being forgiven by God of whatever was in their past as long as life goes on smoothly. As soon as challenges come up, you hear people stirring and scooping up what was forgiven and reviewing the files of ancestral and lineage problems. This is stark ignorance and a cheap way to be hunted down by the wicked.

Many charlatans are always out in the name of prophets

8.2 - *Psalm 51:5*

to take advantage of people and join the kingdom of darkness in hunting people down with their past, making them so paranoid that they can't see the victory Christ already won for them and brought them into as new creations. When you came into the kingdom of God, you came by birth. It is called the new birth which changes your background and lineage from whatever it was into the background and lineage of God's family. The truth is that the enemy will still attempt to hunt you down with memories, experiences, dreams and other tricks there are as much as he possibly can muster. Champions don't allow their past or the past of their parents or lineage to hold them down or back. In this age of global migration and dual citizenship, you should know that no matter how terrible and pariah your nation of natural birth is, once you change citizenship you are given a new passport. You then start experiencing a change in the way you are being treated at the borders of nations who used to be hostile to you, once you present your new passport. If for any reason you are treated unpleasantly now that you are no more a citizen of a pariah nation so to say, you will protest and complain till you get an apology and re-dress. Your complaints and protests won't be on the platform of what citizenship you used to have but of the new found nationality and status. If for any reason you need consular or diplomatic help to get justice, you will seek it from your new influential country and not the old pariah one. You are a new creature as it were in every sense; the old is gone the new has come. The covering over your life is now new. It is therefore not champion –like to be so busy doing deliverances upon deliverances, fighting enemies like the people of the world do in the name of warfare. Most of what people even say in prayer are not little different from what the voodoo men of old used to say. Whereas the nationality has changed, the mind-set has not changed. These are hunted souls and the enemy is succeeding in keeping them busy with fear and condemnations based on their past so they can remain paranoid and hunted all the days of their pilgrimage.

Memory can be mental – This has to do with your storage of information and events in your conscious and sub-conscious mind. Bad memories have a way of coming back in your vulnerable time simply because you are not just dealing with what you have stored in but also what your enemy has kept for playback in his bid to hunt you.

Memory can be experiential – This is about the ways and manners of the life style you have imbibed as nature over time. It serves as a kind of default setting which the enemy wants you to snap back into once you are under stress or in a challenge. All forms of bad addictions fall under this kind of memory.

Memory can be emotional – This is basically the recall of the lasting effects that had been built into your person as expressions of feeling by the past. Capacity to snap and go overboard with anger, depression or any other emotional reaction once a particular issue or event is brought up. This kind of memory creates a pattern of reactions and tensions in relationships, a pattern of reactions whenever faced with challenges.

Whichever one you are dealing with, don't let memory hunt you down. Many can't get over certain bad character or sin because of experiential memory. They have made such way of life their sub-conscious default setting. You need to consciously refute, erase and replace them with the right ones. For example, if unforgiveness and getting even in revenge has been your default setting, it is easy to call for them once offended. Whereas as a kingdom champion, you need to consciously work against it once it shows up until it fades away totally. Nothing hunts like bad memories not replaced with good ones - bad memories of what someone did to you, or on your behalf; bad memory of what you did or should have done, all of which are designed to suck out your energy needed to run and fight in the race of life.

Hunted Within Trouble Without
The battle field of destiny is mostly inside; the enemy hunts people down within first before he starts chasing their stuffs on the outside. Just as salvation proceeds from within, for with the heart man believes unto righteousness before confession leads to salvation. In like manner, destruction and defeats proceeds from the inside. Just as the Holy Spirit does the work of conviction on the inside at salvation, so does the devil the work of condemnation on the inside at destruction. The word "condemnation" is not just a sense of feeling guilty, condemnation also includes excluding oneself from the victory procession and including oneself in the losing camp based on the present or past circumstance. It means to accept qualification for defeat and destruction.

The enemy makes sure such individual loses identity of victory from within. A state of helplessness then sets in till someone who ought to be a kingdom champion starts settling for all manners of diagnosis of man, based on feelings and ignorance.

David was a victim of this working and understands the feeling of it. He knew he had been lied to in the inside and had thus foolishly succumbed to the hunting lies of the enemy of his soul. He knew the only way out is to be liberated from the inside. It is more than a mere event of spiritual goose pimple; it is a process of de-coding and detoxifying the inside of lies and folly, the re-coding of same with truth that will make him wise unto salvation or total emancipation. "Behold you desire truth in the inward parts and in the hidden part you will make me to know wisdom" **[8.3]**. These were the words of a hunted champion who wanted a way out. The truth is what cleanses the inward part not the dream you or a prophet had about you. The word of God is the ultimate truth, the more sure word of prophecy. The word is plural in content but singular in context. The whole context of the word is summarised in Christ as the life that lights men up so that darkness cannot overpower them again **[8.4]**. Any other word, dream, prophecy or interpretations of the bible that places darkness above light is a perversion of the devil sent to hunt men down from the championship they have been called unto. Any anointing so to say that is not empowering the light of life in men but puts men in darkness of fear and paranoia further is not of God. True anointing exposes, elevates and enforces the victories of

8.3 - Psalm 51:6; 8.4 - John 1:1-5

Christ in us. True anointing diminishes and destroys the works and powers of darkness. The job of the wicked is to hunt you and beset you within with lies; it is your responsibility to seek out the truth and get fortified against the hunting wiles of the wicked. Don't store toxins in your inside, get detoxified by light.

Hunted with Offence

The second major hunting weapon of the devil is offence, and it works wonders in defeating champions once allowed within. A famous fight in the world of super heavyweight boxing was the bout of bite between Evander Holyfield and Iron Mike Tyson. The bout was not only famous for the high standing of the two contenders in the boxing world, but also for the dramatic twist to which the contest succumbed. For all purpose and intent, Tyson was offended at what he saw as deliberate head butting by his opponent and the referee's refusal to do something about it over time. It takes time for offence to build up but suddenly like a fermented drink, the outburst that follows is always ridiculous and non-proportional. The rest of that bout is history today as Iron Mike Tyson threw away his chance at glory by biting off the ear lobe of Evander through offence. Many champions have thrown away potential win and trophy in the race of life to offence orchestrated by the kingdom of darkness.

A familiar story of David was his encounter with a diary entrepreneur called Nabal the Calebite and his massive enterprise. Nabal was a man who had succeeded in business and so assumed by David to have possessed human relation skill but unfortunately did not **[8.5]**. We get into offence easily because of the wisdom and loyalty we credit to others by assumptions and later find out not to be there, so the disappointment and then offence. Nabal didn't just hurt David with his unappreciative actions but also with the hurtful words he sent and so the offence just came out like the wave of sea. Thank God for Abigail who spared David of the trouble, and thank God for him listening to wise counsel as well. You have nothing to gain when you live in offence but have much to lose. The Nabal creating offence for you has not much to lose either, so spare yourself the trouble. Nabal was not the principal destiny in the context of the scene, David was and he was the one the offence was directed towards. Many times, champions join losers in petty games of offence and lower themselves into bickering until they themselves are reduced to the losers' status. If David had attacked Nabal, the result could have gone either way as God won't be there fighting a battle of offence with him. If Nabal had heard and ran away, he wouldn't have had time to organise the fatal party that eventually killed him. The worse scenario would have been David adding more enemies by offence to the ones he already had by the reason of whom he was. At long run, once he shunned offence and went about his business, God's hand was given room to work all things together for his good, seeing he loved God and was called according to his purpose.

It is therefore imperative not only to be called into victory and also love God, it is important for us not to tie the hand

8.5 - *1 Samuel 25:1-42*

of heaven that would have worked for us through offence. How can he/she do or say that to me? The truth is the deed is done already; it's time for you to move on. Judas Iscariot is the pioneer saint in the proverbial school of betrayal till date. Jesus clearly knew that Judas was chosen for the betrayal by the enemy so that he, Christ, can be so offended in the betrayal of a friend **[8.6]**. If Christ had succumbed to offence, the victory on the cross would have eluded him and us today. When offence comes, it comes with plenty of woes, it is now your duty to not allow it to rest in you.

Spirit Soul and Body
Offence weakens the spirit of champions; it reduces the capacity for reception of what heaven is saying seriously. The familiar story of Elisha shows what offence can do **[8.7]**. Elisha was obviously offended with the king of Israel for the obvious reason of the former not walking in the way of the Lord. No matter the excuse, for every action there will be an equal or unequal and opposite reaction. Once the offence set in, Elisha's capacity to hear and see into the mind of God aright was compromised. They had to get someone singing not because God couldn't speak without the songs but Elisha needed the door of his spirit to be re-opened, as it had been locked through offence. Nothing worthy in the kingdom of God can be done or initiated in offence. The way of the enemy limiting any vision is to sow seeds of offence in it. It is therefore possible to go into offence and block out the hand of God on our own life simply by allowing the obvious wrong doings of others in the kingdom to put us in the position of

8.6 - Luke 17:1; *8.7* - 2 Kings 3:5-15

offence. This, I believe, is one of the reasons Jesus discouraged the judgement of others by us. It is easy to slip into offence in the name of standing against what is wrong. I am not advocating compromise or discouraging standing for that which is pure and true. Even if you will have to part way with someone in a vision or association to pursue another line, don't let the enemy sow the seed of offence in your heart. Surely, offensive words and actions will be sown as seeds, but don't offer the soil of your heart as a breeding ground; they will only bear fruits of woes.

Offence corrupts the soul, which is the centre of your intellect (mind), will and emotion. Once offence is taken in, sound reasoning will be compromised, emotional outburst and eventual wrong use of will in making and taking wrong decisions and steps are inevitable. Wise and smart people make sloppy and foolish decisions and take wrong steps once they are in offence. People will start wondering how he or she can do or say that. People behave out of character when they are simply reactionary rather than being actioner or even pro-active. They do and say things as reactions to fight back at what others are saying and doing. They don't say and do because that is who they are and what they intend to do. Many visions and pursuits are simply reactional to someone's and not an original pursuit of heaven's intent and purpose.

Once the spirit is weakened and soul perverted by offence, the body will follow suit in weakness and perversion alike. Sickness and diseases can easily set in when offence is in place; the devourer can easily get a foothold in material wealth once offence is in place. God told Job to come out of offence against all his friends for all they had done and said to him by praying for them. Job 42:10. Once Job prayed for them, and was free of offence within, his captivity turned without. His money was brought back from the hand of the devourer, his marriage restored and he had kids. His body was healed and life was worth living for him again.

It is a Plague
Do not pray against offence coming as they will surely come no matter how hard you pray. Jesus said it will surely come as we saw earlier. Your job is to avoid offence like a plague. Do all you can to sanctify the Lord in your own heart in the face of offence and offensive people. Saul became demoniac once he slipped into offence through envy. Don't envy anyone, good or bad when they prosper. God knows better to have given them whatever they have, even if you feel they don't deserve it. Our opinion is literally secondary when it comes to God blessing another person, so if he chooses to bless the one we term as underserving, let it be. Even if you chose not to acknowledge or celebrate with them, still watch your heart for offence. Below is a great admonition from a man who saw it all in the school of offence but rose above them all:

"For the eyes of the Lord is over the righteous and his ears are opened unto their prayers; but the face of the Lord is against those who do evil. And who is he who will harm you if you become followers of

what is good? But even if you should suffer for righteousness sake, you are blessed. And don't be afraid of their threats nor be troubled, but sanctify the Lord God in your hearts and always ready to give a defence to everyone who asks you a reason for the hope that is in you with meekness and fear." [8.8].

Hunted by Distractions

The final hunting weapon of the wicked we shall be looking at for now is the weapon of distraction. Once the enemy can't hunt you down within through your past and can't get you disqualified through offence, all that is left for him is to try and distract you on the tract of race. Distractions can come in sin or pleasure; it can come in challenges or victories alike. Whatever takes your eyes off the goal of conquests is a distraction. Even when it is wearing a religious garment, the sole aim of distraction is to slow you down or put you off course all together.

Speed is of no use in a race once you head the wrong direction; distraction compromises direction and makes all effort of little or no value. There are many spectators in the race of life than runners; they are in to catch fun and make some noise and not to win any prize. As a runner who is up for the prize, you need focus borne out of blindness to the sights and deafness to the noise around. During the year 2012 Olympic held in the city of London, a top athlete had a plastic bottle thrown at him for whatever reason by a spectator. The athlete didn't even pay enough attention as to notice such distraction, he was too busy focusing on the race for prize and surely he

8.8 - *1 Peter 3:12-16*

won the prize. The legendary prime minister of the Great Britain during the Second World War, Winston Churchill has this to say *"You will never reach your destination if you stop and throw stones at every dog that barks".* It takes losing the election to form the opposition party in politics; losers are always the loudest critics, and criticism can be a distraction. Human expectations of you can be a distraction at times too. You need to know what you are constituted and packaged for rather than what anyone else sets before you as goal.

Save your Breath

It is the judicious and conservative management of your resources that makes a wise virgin of you. If the waiting for the groom is longer than envisaged, you must be judicious not to run out of fuel and be caught unaware. New Year resolutions are not enough to deliver your destiny; staying in focus year in year out is what will do. It is not enough to be zealous at the beginning of a venture, but to last in breath is what will deliver the trophies therein. Don't waste your emotional currency on worthless transactions; save your breath for the real deal. Many will come to steal your breath and energy; don't give them room for once. The rule of thumb is to avoid such. There is no other way than to avoid vision, emotional and strength depleting associations and companies no matter how costly it seems. You can either pay that price now and win back your vision, strength and emotion for profitable investments or lose them all in the long run and be bankrupt in the market place of life when such capital are needed.

Stay in the Flock
One of the major but simple ways of hunting by the enemy of your soul is the way of isolation. Distractions are aimed at taking you out of the company of champions and isolating you for onslaught in your vulnerable moment. Men who are promiscuous always isolate the good girls from their good friends and families in order to take advantage of them; isolated from second opinions, isolated from unbiased and unclouded judgement. Such people are isolated from godly counsels and then taken prey like a chicken to be devoured of all flesh. Before faith fails, one has to be distracted from the company of faith builders and faith strengtheners. The first step lions take when attacking a flock of other animals they want for prey is to distract and isolate one of them. Once isolated, the deal is done. Even if it is an elephant, it will soon come down in the face of relentless onslaught of bites and claws. Satan is likened to a hunting lion when it comes to his plan for a champion like you. Part of the sobriety and vigilance required from you is to avoid being distracted from the right company.

Jesus in several of his teachings on finances said the reason why people are denied the kingdom wealth is because they are being distracted from the kingdom focused race by the cares of this world. Distractions by the thoughts of what to eat, drink and wear have blindfolded them from doing the major thing and so robbed them of being fed and clothed from heaven **[8.9]**.

8.9 - *Luke 6:30-32*

PRIEST AND KING

One of the reasons God goes through several thousands of people and singles a few out for extra ordinary feat is so that such ones as have found great mercy and grace can be examples of His goodness, longsuffering and love. The love and longsuffering of God are the basis of Him seeking reconciliations with those that are ignorant and errant of the way. God therefore seeks men who are made strong and not those who are strong by themselves. He seeks those with a sense of awe for the honour of being called and not those who see the call unto the winning life as an entitlement.

Priestly Champion
There are only two reigning platforms for saints here on earth; we either reign as priests or as kings. These are the only two packages in which our reining grace came. Kingdom champions don't reign in life because they are doctors, lawyers, architects, business men or women; we don't reign in life because we are teachers, pastors, apostles prophets or evangelist and such. Believers don't reign in life because of their college background, race, tribe or vocations. We don't reign in life because we are in show-business, sports or any other popular vocation

there are. Individual vocation can be a channel of expression unto winning but no one wins in God's kingdom because of what he or she does as vocation or by natural birth. The platform of winning is impartial; God made all his children priests and kings at redemption. God knows we won't all come from same race or tribe, he knows we won't be doing same things as vocation. Neither are we all going to be naturally endowed in same way and proportion. But the good news is that God didn't package our reigning in any of such unequal platform.

"And they sang a new song saying, you are worthy to take the book and open its seals. For you have redeemed us to God by your blood out of every tribe and tongue and people and nation, and have made us kings and priests to our God, and we shall reign on earth" [9.1].

The above quotation was lifted from the prayers of the saints or believers which ascended to heaven as incense filling the golden bowls of the seraphims' harps. I am sure believers were praying all manner of prayers about reigning in life and being the best God has created them to be but it was this profound revelation in prayer that found its way into the harp for all to hear and celebrate the risen lamb of God with. They affirmed believers' call unto dominion through our office as priests and kings, and those alone.

The priest in question is the priest of blessedness after the order of Christ Jesus whose priesthood office was shadowed by Melchisedec. This is the priesthood shared

9.1 - Revelation 5:8-10

by clergy and laity; the priesthood is on the pulpits and pews alike; the priesthood of saints is universal and ubiquitous without hierarchy. The priesthood garment is the righteousness of Christ that covers us all; it's not the ceremonial garment of intimidation adopted by any denomination. Believers' priesthood is not in the Aaronic order; it has nothing to do with Levi. We are descendants of Christ and not of Aaron. If anyone is therefore busy with all the ceremonial washings and wearing in the Levitical priesthood, it is a mere waste of time and waste of grace of reigning in life brought to us all by Christ Jesus. There truly might be a few overlap in the duty of Levitica's and Christ's priesthoods, but they are not the same. Whereas the Levitical priesthood is an office for a selected few in a selected tribe of a selected nation, New Testament priesthood is for everyone from every tribe in every nation who believes in and is saved by Christ Jesus. I am laying this emphasis so that saints don't get robbed of their blessing and dominion by the laws and deceitful craftiness of men who love using office as a pedestal of robbery. I am also laying this emphasis so that you don't count yourself out of the race for winning as a priestly champion because you didn't realise that you are one of such.

Priests are chosen first to minister to God, and then minister to men in things that pertain to God. They are chosen to offer both gifts and sacrifices towards heaven and bring compassion and blessing towards the earth. Priests are chosen to heal the ignorant of their ignorance and bestow strength unto the feet that are turned out of the way.

Minister of Better Covenant
The concept of ministering stems from waiting on a superior to serve the person in all capacities, especially running errands and doing all their menials jobs. In like manner, all kingdom champions are sent to wait on God as priests to run errands for him and do the entire kingdom's menial jobs. Jesus was portrayed to us a minister of the better covenant; and he came up with better results indeed. But how else did he go about it but by stooping low to pick up the menial assignment of redemption on earth on behalf of the Godhead. He was the strong one who took on weakness so as to make the weak us strong.

God wants you to get better results beyond what your wildest imagination can fathom, simply because you are part of the priesthood of Christ, even the priesthood of the better covenant. You therefore need to wait on God or serve him in one capacity or the other. Serving God is vast and all-encompassing but one important way of doing so is to serve in the house of God (Church) and or in other kingdom fronts (missions). Serving is not the same as having a title or ordination ceremonies into positions which many think is an end in the kingdom business. With or without an office or position, you are meant to be available for all kinds of assignments in the kingdom. This should be done without seeking material reward as the motivation; it should be done without seeking visibility or human praise. David was such a man who was ready to be a door keeper in the house of God as part of his ministering to the Lord. No wonder he was such one as can supply enough gold for the building of God's temple from his personal treasure without going bankrupt **[9.2]**.

The other way of ministering to God as priests is by offering the fruits of our lips unto him as sacrifice of praise. Every New Testament priest is expected to do this without fear or wrath. Praise, prayers and thanksgiving are the fruits of our lips which must be offered continually as incense and burnt sacrifice day and night. Beyond intercession for others or requesting for something for ourselves or our loved ones, prayer is a service all saints must be rendering without ceasing. The fear of the devil and being paranoid about evil must not be the reason behind our prayers, we must pray as champions because we are priests. David prayed, David sang and David danced; all unto the Lord. He was a man wearing ephod (the priestly garment of his days) and so he saw ministering unto the Lord as a must do assignment **[9.3]**.

We also need to be conscious of our calling as priests in ministering to people. We owe all mankind our ministry of priesthood. We owe the unsaved ones the gospel of Christ Jesus so they may see light. The western world and so many nations of the world make it look like a taboo to preach the gospel of the Lord Jesus to others. They make it look too intrusive into others' affairs, but we can never be politically correct about preaching the gospel.

9.2 - Psalms 84:10; *9.3* - Psalms 27:6-8

God has given the office of the priest to us and one of the jobs of the priest is to reconcile the errant ones back unto God. We must use every platform of lifting in life given us as tools of evangelism; it is not priest-like for saints to keep quiet about their faith in Christ because they don't want to rock the social boat.

Kingdom champions are called as priests to minister grace unto one another as well; in every situation two must always be better than one. If well understood, you will know that you are called to strengthen other saints and not to weaken them. Priests are sent to help the ignorant and the ones turned out of the way, not to make them more ignorant or turn further away into the bush of perdition. You can't be competing with and cutting down your fellow saint whom you have been sent to as priest to minister the grace of heaven unto. You can't be secretly happy when a saint falls or fails in life; you will be abusing your priesthood office by doing and feeling so. You are called to affirm other champions and make them feel appreciated, not converting their gold to brass with some condescending words or attitudes. God can never and will never be the God of only your denomination, dreams, visions and convictions. God is vast and is the father of all who call on Him through Christ Jesus our Lord. Get used to a large family with all kinds of men and women making up the household. It takes a broad mind to walk on a narrow path; you can't be narrow-minded because the kingdom path of life is narrow. You have to see beyond your own little self and preference; you have to see beyond your personal comfort and aggrandisement. You can't afford to be so consumed with your own needs and desires with the assumption that the kingdom of God exists solely for that. Kingdom champions are mission minded, they know and live like people who are on mission to get something accompanied for the king. It is a "must-be-done" king's assignment and nothing is primary to that. They don't allow career pursuits, challenges of life, pleasure of success, social justice or political movements to erode mission off their minds.

Kingdom champions are raised as priests, a people ready to use their exaltations in life as pedestals of sacrificial ministering to God and mankind to the glory of the one who honoured them by calling them unto glory and virtue.

Royal All The Way
Sleeping or awake, a lion is a lion and would never be called any other thing; so is your status as a king eternal no matter what you are going through. No matter your vocation, you are called a king sent to show off the glory of the King of kings. Jesus is also the King of us kingdom kings as a sign of fraternity not merely the king of the worldly kings as a sign of superiority and dominion.

In the Old Testament, the king is mostly involved in the expeditions and enterprise of war and kingdom trading. They wage war to enrich their own kingdom and also send out emissaries on seas to trade and bring in fortunes into the kingdom. The activities of priests are strictly restricted within the temple and the temple frontiers, but kings go beyond that. Some of us will reign in life through priestly platforms of the royal priesthood, while others will do so through the kingly platforms of same. Simply put, some will have the champions in them evolve through ministry while others will have same through industry. Whichever path God wants you to take, our royal priesthood is more of who we are than what we do as vocation.

Much Business

Champions are not mere dreamers, they pursue. They are men and women who don't just sit down wishing and waiting for success to happen. It is common among non-achievers to always attribute all success and achievements to luck and or crookedness. To them, the achievers are either lucky or dubious. What a way to remain a failure in life! It takes throwing yourself into it to be counted in. Kingdom champions are not idlers. No dream of significance can be realised by mere dreaming it and talking it idly. It takes running for the vision to speak, even at the appointed time **[9.4]**. Writing the vision is good, waiting on the appointed time is fantastic, but the vision will only speak for whoever runs with it. Appointed time will only come to those who pursue; it is only set along the path of pursuit for runners to catch up with. The church world in particular is full of talkers, analysers and commentators. Unfortunately, nothing significant speaks for any of those. Vision only speaks for runners. Running is the only way to open the mouth of

9.4 - Habakkuk 2:2

vision and give it a voice to speak at the appointed time.

May your God given vision not be dumb and voiceless as a result of not running with it!

Kings are not mere talkers; kings are given to enterprise. They send ships on water and prosecute wars; they don't sit down idling and feasting. David was a doing and a go-getter king. The only time he had a serious moral problem on the throne was when he joined mere talkers to stay back at home having fun when he ought to be out there warring. Financial prosperity is not a mystery beyond the blessing of God resting on the hand of man to produce supernatural result in wealth. There must be something you are doing; there must be something you are delivering as goods or services for money to come back to you in return as reward. Many in the body of Christ use the bulk of their times to criticise and analyse others who are prospering and yet they wonder why they are not in the league of the very prosperous. There is no vacuum in life; you get rewarded in what you dedicate your time, energy and thoughts unto. The question will be to ask yourself, "how much will this adventure deliver into my hand of all I dream of?" God himself believes in reward - he is the rewarder of them that diligently seek him - the word of God says. Life itself is wired with various reward systems. Athletes and sport personalities whose performances attract crowd and huge revenues seemingly get paid ridiculous money for few hours of display. But the reality is that the few hours in public display are products of several hours behind the scene in preparations and discipline. Some of the casual observers of life are furious and yelling at how obscene it is to pay someone such a huge sum while many people are hungry. It is sadly understandable to hold such sentiments, but no one gets paid for being furious as such.

Kingdom champions don't just talk of what they wish for; they do what it takes to get it done. Sitting down in pleasure and waiting for God to get the business done is a short cut for princes to be walking on feet while servants ride on horses. Prayer will never do what has been assigned for hard work to do and vice versa. It is the responsibility of a kingdom champion to know the difference and then align accordingly. Solomon, the son of David has this to say on how real dreams find expression in the hands of champions and vice versa. "Because of laziness the building decays, and through idleness of hand the house leaks" **[9.5]**.

Custodian of Wealth

Kings splendour and treasures are the true reflection of the kingdom wealth; they are responsible for how wealthy or otherwise the kingdom is. Kingdom champions are supposed to reflect the wealth of God kingdom in one hand and also be the custodian of same here on earth to accomplish the king's purpose. It is an irony when the world that claims to be fighting poverty descends on the Church in vicious criticism when the Church does same fighting through financial prosperity. The kingdom of God is a wealthy kingdom by all means and in every sense of it. Kingdom champions are the

9.5 - Ecclesiastes 10:18

custodians of the wealth therein here on earth. When champions go to the market place of life to engage themselves in productive ventures, God causes the blessing of heaven to rest on it and make the blessing to produce riches in the hands of his people.

Having been blessed thus, it is pertinent to know what the purposes thereof are. The Lord blesses for us to enjoy, for us to help the poor and to make financial resources available in the Church to preach the gospel. David made provision for the building of God's temple from the plenty in his hands, even though he wouldn't be the one receiving the glory for building it **[9.6]**. Don't by any means think that the gold or silver in your hand is for mere personal adornment; God has need of it. He has need of it to help the poor and needy; he has need of it in the Church and mission fields to build His kingdom. Kingdom champions don't only build God's house but also encourage others to join in doing so. I have heard many people talk down the Church and yet they are believers. Champions don't behave that way. Heaven won't drop the dollars and pound sterling, or whatever currency you spend from the sky into the kingdom. He will channel them through the kings by the way of productive ventures they engage in.

War for Peace
Kings fight wars that peace may reign in the land of their domain, and kingdom champions are not different. Fight a good fight of faith is a word of advice for soldiers, because all kings of the kingdom of God are first soldiers

9.6 - *1 Chronicles 22:14-19*

of righteousness. We fight to enforce the peace of the liberty wherein Christ has called us unto. So many forces and issues will arise in our lives and territories to rob us of the peace of the kingdom in us. Our response is not to sit still weeping and saying we don't want trouble. Our response is to stand up and confront the adversary. In like manner, when human agents are set to rob us of the kingdom peace by sowing all manners of evil seeds of discord and contention, it is our duty to rise up and confront them, thereby enforcing the peace of the kingdom. Many times, we need to fight for the rest wherewith we are been made to rest. God gave David rest round about because David fought when he needed to fight.

Every king's kingdom is intact and the subject safe until a stronger king comes and overpowers him to plunder his subject. Therefore, kingdom champions can't afford to be weaklings, watching the enemy plundering their territories. The meekest state of Christ was that of a Lion, so his kingdom's territorial integrity remains intact without an iota of compromise.

Decreeing Justice

It is no more news that we live in a wicked world; kingdom kings are therefore set on thrones so that their eyes can scatter evil perpetually. Kings don't joke with words. No matter how powerful a king is, the dissemination of the ruler-ship is by the words of his decree. **Where the word of a king is there is power, and who may say to him what are you doing** [9.7]. The

9.7 - Ecclesiastes 8:4

power of a king is as far as his word reaches; it is only the spoken word of the king that is immune to challenges. The reference didn't say "who may say to him what are you thinking". Thoughts of dominion within a king's heart must be so abundant that they will be crystallised to words of decree which can't be challenged by any mutinous force. God has the capacity to be anything and still get the result He wants anyway, but He refused to be an introvert when His creation was challenged by darkness and voidness after the beginning. God spoke out that light must be and light was. God has the capacity to think it and get it done but He doesn't want us to operate like that, so therefore he showed us the example of doing it. Kings don't suggest their dominion, they decree it.

David was not an introvert when it came to matters of dominion. He never kept quiet on what he wanted to see done by light against the darkness of his own days. He was the one who admonished the redeemed of the lord to say so even when it sounds strange and unpopular **[9.8]**. The scheme of the kingdom of this world is to silence us about the all-conquering power of our faith. A king must not keep mute in the face of Goliath or else he will keep coming back to harass day and night. Goliath of Gath had been talking loud against the whole Israel for forty days and nights, but the day David spoke up against Goliath in reply was the last day we heard Goliath's voice among the living. You can't afford to keep mute. Political correctness across the world is tailored towards making saints keep mute. The few amongst us who are the

9.8 - Psalms 107:2

speaking ones are placed on the hot seat and under serious scrutiny so we can keep quiet, but the good news is that we aren't going to keep quiet. Our God is well able to do all we say; He is able to do and He will do them, but even if He refuses to do them, we will still not keep quiet one bit.

Kingdom champions are kings and kings are not flippant with words. They decree justice and release virtue (power) by words. The kingdom we represent on earth is the kingdom of purity, power and prosperity, and we can't be forced to stop saying so. We can't stop saying the words of righteousness because the world feels uncomfortable that we call sin what they call choice and fun. We can't stop talking healing and health through the stripes of Jesus because everyone is not yet healed and someone might therefore feel pressured and desperate or disappointed. We can't stop talking it loud that we serve a God who is able to make all grace abound towards us, help us have the sufficiency of all things and yet make us abound in good works. We can't stop saying so because someone will feel we are worldly or will feel we are fleecing people with the good news. We can afford to do a lot of things, but the kings in Zion can't afford to stop decreeing justice. The mountains and lowlands must hear our roaring from near and afar; the look and sneer in their faces must not intimidate us. Part of our battles is the battle of words which we must not shy away from but prosecute with all diligence till the earth is filled with the glory of the knowledge of our God as the water covers the sea.

Kingdom champions don't even joke in words with defeat. They don't joke with dying young, being sick, poor and all the idle words the people of the world find funny at the expense of destiny. Kings don't talk loosely; they pick and choose their words with wisdom of their kingdom in order not to create a crack in their defence.

Stop saying what you don't mean because of what you are going through. It is carnal to talk for mere emotional rush after which the word leaves your teeth on edge like sore grapes. Even if other believers are saying such ungracious words about their own situations in the name of prayer or under any guise, don't join them. Don't join multitude in doing that which is wrong. Champions don't talk fear and defeat no matter how much the battle is set in array. When the whole army of Israel, including Saul on whose head the crown was temporarily were talking fear and defeat, the only true king of the kingdom among them was David who was talking victory all the way. No wonder he was soon crowned accordingly in order to preserve the integrity of the kingdom victory. Stop shifting the victory into the enemy's territory with your words; kings rule by words.

Chapter Ten

WINNING HERE AND THERE

God's kingdom is everlasting, and so is our reign. Our conquest is eternal just as the plan and purpose of God for us is eternal. Eternity doesn't start at death for us as saints, it starts the day we received Christ into our heart. Eternal life came into our spirit at the moment of salvation, not when we die and go to literal heaven. Eternal life is so called not because of its length but because of the quality. The longevity of the life is not what made it eternal life but the quality thereof. It is the quality that makes it impossible to have an end. In like manner, the quality of our conquest through Jesus Christ is such that our winning starts now and continues life without end.

The Now Life

Religion has painted a very awkward picture of the Christian faith to the world and thereby giving the world a very serious platform of fighting the Church when they see us doing well and even better than them here on earth. The picture is that all the good and precious things the kingdom of heaven has to offer us are only available to us when we get to heaven while we just struggle and get by here till we get there. What can be further from the truth of the kingdom than this lie of the devil? It is a profane fable that is worthy of only rejection and nothing more. We can't separate our lives into compartments as the world and religion wants us to do. We can't compartmentalise our lives into spiritual life, marital life, financial life and so on and so forth. The world, with the help of religion wants us to do this so that they can then determine what and where Christ's redemptive works affect and benefits believers. It can't be so, champion; your life is just one and the all demarcations therein are man-made.

***But reject profane and old wives' fables and exercise yourself towards godliness. For bodily exercise profits little but godliness is profitable for all things, having the promise of the life that now is and that which is to come* [10.1]**.

The above statement is the ultimate truth of the winning territories of the kingdom champions. They are not some beaten and battered soldiers who are so ravaged that they barely made it to the finish line at the pearl gate, as religion says it. Basking in defeats here on earth is not a guarantee for glory in heaven. In fact, fighting a good fight here is part of the pre-requisite for the glory there.

David did maximize his potentials and possibilities while here on earth as a champion, for he knew that there is not another chance afterwards. It is therefore needful for you to squeeze the last drop off the golden chance God has given you now. Don't suspend living till someone else shows up in your life as spouse. Live and glorify God with your life now no matter what the culture calls life and

10.1 - *1 Timothy 4:7-8*

living and how far you are from the expectation thereof. Live and make life count for as long as you have your breath. Don't live in regrets and illusion of yesterday that has gone or didn't happen as you had wished or planned. Champions see each day as the day that the Lord has made and they will rejoice and be glad in it as much as they can.

Everything you need for this present life is already made available in Christ; it is high time to search the key to unlock them out **[10.2]**. All things that pertain to life here was not said to be given us by the knowledge of those things which were given to us as we have been told by preachers and teachers for long. We are given access to these things through the knowledge of God and of Christ, we were told. The difference in just having the knowledge of things given and having the knowledge of him who gave them is enormous; it makes the difference between those who are dreaming of having and those who have eventually. One can know all God can do and all that Christ has done and still not enjoy them. The beginning of triumph for kingdom champions in enjoying the great and precious promises or packages of heaven on earth is to have a knowing of the one who made the packages available. It is therefore not good enough to know all the formulae of the kingdom's financial packages; it will only breed greed at best or create frustrations while trying to make the word work by all means. The delivery key is to have a knowing of the one who has called us into such a good financial package. It is not even sufficient to know about God to enjoy the kingdom package, because one can

10.2 - *2 Peter 1:2 -3*

know about someone without meeting the person even once.

To know God is a language of intimacy, God wants the holy intimacy of cooperating with the divine to happen in our life, so we can enjoy all things that pertain to life and godliness. It is good to have deep and broad knowledge of all subject matters that have to do with our lives here on earth, but the knowledge of God is the platform of delivery in the kingdom here on earth. Reading the biography or even the autobiography of someone does not give you the authority to lay claim of knowing the person. The bible is not God's autobiography that we are just expected to read and know about God and then extract whichever formulae we think we need to get whatever our lusts desire here on earth. Not at all, the bible was given as light so we can see the way towards God for personal relationship.

The truths of the kingdom are packaged in mystery for our glory; the key to unlock them is the key of intimacy with the one who packaged the truth in mystery. Jesus knew the bible was going to be written and published in such a way that every literate person can read it. Yet, he said we can't afford to go into searching it without another comforter like him who will relate with us on the platform of all truths. God wants relationship rather than head knowledge; to know God is not same as to know God's book per say. To know God is to settle down for a relationship, a continuous and fruitful one for that matter. David read the bible of his days but as a champion of the kingdom, he did more than reading. David related with God, he pressed his ear to the chest of God by every means he knew to know the voice of God. He fixed his gaze so much on the beauty of God that he soon lost sight of the ugliness around him and started telling others to taste and see that the Lord is good. Chasing any other thing at the expense of seeking a deep relationship with God is idolatry and the result is always a chasing of wind and a denial of such at the end of the day. People who relate deeply with God can't deny his power to make well and bless all round. They rather affirm it and stand by it. You can't be relating with the Almighty God and be affirming weakness, sickness, lack and all the ugly works of the devil. Your affirmation is the true reflection of your realities and determines your ultimate experience. Are you with God? What do you see around him? What forms your realities in the life you live now? These are all questions that border on intimacy with God.

The World to Come

Kingdom champions live the life of God in them in the now but they don't live just for now. It is needful to know that the headquarters of our kingdom is not here on earth. We are here on an assignment and we shall depart once we are done with our own part of the transaction. It is also needful to know that not only must we strive not to lose our pass into glory but to also know that we shall account for our sojourn here unto the master when we get back home. True kingdom champions can never make their treasures here and still leave them here where they can be corrupted or stolen. They have their hearts planted in heaven and so there they invest the good treasures of their time, talents and other resources while still here on earth.

David was troubled at one point in his life by the relative comfort the sinners seemed to be enjoying at the expense of the saints, and he was almost asking himself what the point was of being godly. Then he went into the presence of God and God had to teach him this profound truth. *"The sinners can afford to spend and have it all here, but you can't".* Afterwards, his prayer language changed, and he started seeing things on earth with the other side of eternity in perspective **[10.3]**. You can't drink all they drink and sniff all they sniff into their orifices; sleep with all they sleep with and marry all they marry, champion! You can't even spend your time the ways they do, neither can you live just to please yourself and your fleshly desires as they do. You are on duty here as a soldier. They don't have a master to report to in heaven but you do. They are on spending spree, you are in investment mission; you are here to invest all of yourself into the kingdom of God like a seed so as to reap the peaceable fruits of glory in the world to come.

The word of Christ is that you can't afford to win here at the expense of winning there in eternity. Winning here is good, winning here and there is better and the real deal **[10.4]**. Life in God is about profiting and Christ said it is an incomparable loss and not profiting to gain on earth and lose out in heaven. Don't gain friend here at the expense of there. Don't gain money here at the expense of there;

10.3 - *Psalms 73:22-23;* **10.4** - *Matthew 16:24-27*

don't gain fame here at the expense of eternity.

Friend of the Groom
Every true kingdom champion loves the master of the house - Jesus Christ. They know it was his conquest that made us triumphant and not our wits. Those who love Christ love his Church and what he stands for, and will do all within their reach to seek the prosperity of his kingdom. Those who love Christ now also love and look forward to his appearing in the last day. They don't get so caught up with the activities in this present world as to forget the coming back of the master of the house **[10.5]**. Those that love and look forward to the coming back of Christ in his glory don't sit down and fold their hands and take up the roles of kingdom commentators and critics; they keep fighting the good fight of keeping the faith. They keep discovering and pursuing their course on earth till they finish exploring same in grand style and the winning way. Those who are truly busy fighting and winning in the kingdom love the appearing of the master and those who love the appearing of the master are busy fighting and winning. David was one of us who loved Christ whom he had not seen. He so much made friend in his heart with Christ that he spoke about Christ in prophecies much more than virtually anyone in the Old Testament, even those who clearly occupied the office of prophets. David was a friend of the house of the Lord, a friend of the people of the Lord and a friend of the assignments of building the Lord's kingdom. Friendship is based on mutual understanding, as two can only work

10.5 - 2 Timothy 4:7-8

together if they agree. The Lord knew and understood the needs of David, and David in turn chose to understand the ways of the Lord.

It is instructive for us to befriend him who died for us on the platform of friendship and rose again to make us the champions we are in his kingdom.

Chapter Eleven

WINNING LEGACIES

God raises people up in their own generations not just for the fun of raising people; He raises champions to impart generational lessons or legacies on their own generations and the ones to come after. The kingdom of God here on earth for now is not going to be for ever. Timing and seasons are therefore so relevant to all operations of the kingdom now. Instead of repeating the same lesson over and again, God will rather that His people learn from those who had gone ahead and so get more perfected. The invisible things of God are only made known through what He has made. He so told generations after Abraham to look at him and learn the art of trusting for turnarounds in whatever they are going through **[11.1]**. In like manner, God will love your winning in life to further establish the kingdom way of raising men and women of destinies. This singular reason is why many of us get so frustrated in life when things don't go our way initially.

Generational Blessing
Whatever good thing God does for His people, the same is the least He wants their children and many generations after them to enjoy and improve on in their walk with Him. Kingdom champions are not just concerned about

11.1 - Isaiah 51:1-2

sending their children to good schools and buying them the best toys and garments in town; they are more concerned about leaving them on the pathway of the blessing and leaving the consciousness of the blessing in them. Solomon attested to the fact that if by any means he stayed on the right path, it was because he obliged the words of his father **[11.2]**. Every king in Israel and Judah that walked the right path was said to have walked the way of David, and the ones who strayed were said to have departed from the way of their father, David.

God kept telling the children of Israel that would inherit Canaan not only to bequeath material blessings to their children, but for them to bequeath a legacy of godliness to them as well. God said they should not hide the source of their material blessings, which is the blessing of the Lord, from their children. They were commanded to tell them how they were not born into money but how God lifted them and helped them greatly because they loved and followed Him as the God of their own fathers too. The present day media and governments are not obliged to show your children the way of God, you are. The media and governments would rather we don't mention God nor teach our children the way of God. They deploy all manner of schemes to prosecute such evil crusade, but we owe God, His kingdom and our posterity the obligation no matter how politically incorrect we are tagged. The media and modern day governments don't mind if we expose our children to alcohol, drug and illicit sex but they mind if we expose them to the bible and prayers and other things that have to do with godliness and

11.2 - *Proverbs 4:3-6*

righteousness. Children are not the government's or community's heritage; they are the heritage of God and the Lord alone. They are given to us by God to raise for Him, and we have all the duty in the world to determine the path we want our children to thread. Every kingdom champion will stand by this simple rule and dare the consequence till the will of God is established in their children. God didn't give us those children to be raised as drug addicts, alcoholics or sexually perverted and ungodly non-believers. He gave them to us to be raised in the consciousness of the covenant of Abraham through our Lord Jesus. We must not be too educated and sophisticated for the covenant.

Helped by Heaven

Kingdom champions are not strong in themselves; they are men and women with flaws, limitations and inadequacies. Part of the legacies of Kingdom champions is that we don't just see heaven as our retirement home after here; we see heaven as a place to lean upon and look up to for help even right now. It was David who wrote the famous Psalm 121 where he affirmed that his help was coming from heaven (above) and thus the presence of covering shade over his life day and night. The consciousness of heaven as the source of help was ingrained in the lineage of David that generations after him made it a practice and confession to look heaven-ward in time of trouble. Asa was some generations down the line from David and hear what he said. *"...It is nothing for you to help whether with many or with those who have no power, help us O Lord our God for we rest on you..."* **[11.3]**. This was an extract in the middle of the prayer Asa prayed when faced with a very challenging situation as a king. Jehoshaphat was also another one down the line of David; hear what he had to say too. *"... For we have no power against this great multitude that is coming against us, nor do we know what to do but our eyes are upon you..."* **[11.4]**. This was an extract from the prayer of King Jehoshaphat when faced with daunting task of life and could not match up by himself.

Don't hide the secret of divine help from your children and followers. Let them know and imbibe the truth of relying on heaven when all resources on earth have failed. There is nothing to be shameful about in God. To thank God publicly for achievement now sounds offensive but kingdom champions must not shy away from their reliance on heaven for help.

Leader of Company

One crucial legacy that must be left behind by those champions made strong in the kingdom is for the generations coming to know that every kingdom champion is a leader of a company and not a solo fighter. In as much as we face challenges of life with personal responsibilities, we should still acknowledge the fact that we are in a company and leading a company. The glory of triumph in the kingdom is therefore not a personal trophy to aggrandise. David made sure that the names and exploits of his great men were recorded for posterity. From the onset when they were some bunch of truants and indebted and dis-contented men to when

11.3 - *2 Chronicles 11:11;* ***11.4*** - *2 Chronicles 20:12*

they started lifting up swords to take lands and nation, David didn't deny them their place in glory and history **[11.5]**. On many occasions, God will choose a set-man or a leader to lead the company in the kingdom endeavour. It must be pretty clear that all the reward and glory of the company triumph will never and must never go to the set-man or set-woman. There is no one man army than a metaphorical saying. Killing Goliath by David was the beginning of Israel's triumph over the Philistines, not the end thereof. The battle went all night till the alien army fled before that army of the Lord. Even the Lord Jesus who is captain of the host of heaven won't come alone in his second coming; the Lord shall come with thousands and tens of thousands of his saints to execute judgement on the kingdom of darkness **[11.6]**. Individual contribution to the company may be different in size and gravity but it is still a company; everyone must be accorded his or her due portion of the spoil. Christianity is not a gathering of lone stars but a company of morning stars who love shining together. One lone shining star with millions of weaklings as followers is not the kingdom of God's pattern, one strong leader and several battered followers is not the kingdom pattern. It is the will of God for all His children to grow in strength and manifest the glory inside of them within their company, without competition or rank breaking.

11.5 - *1 Chronicles 11:1-47;* ***11.6*** - *Jude 14-15*

Chapter Twelve

MADE STRONG

In rounding off this book, I will love to emphasise that fact that kingdom champions are made strong by a higher power and not really strong in their own selves. Jesus emphasised the place of strength among the kingdom champions when he gave an illustration of a strong man's house which remains intact as long as nothing stronger than him comes upon him to bind and loot him **[12.1]**. We live in a world where strength counts a lot. Survival in our world is still of the fittest till the kingdom comes. Solomon, the son of David must have learnt from his father that the days of adversities are inevitable. He knew that the presence of adversary is also inevitable but that failure in the face of adversity is avoidable. All that is needed is just sufficient strength and all will be well **[12.2]**. Whether you want to cry or throw some tantrum, that's fine but just be strong in the day of adversity. Victory in the face of challenges requires corresponding strength. It is not strange to have no strength of yours but it is unwise not to employ higher strength. You can only joy in your infirmity when you have discovered and appropriated the strength of the Lord. Joying in weakness and infirmity while you haven't sought and appropriated heaven's strength made available in grace is not only unwise, it is an express invitation to defeat of disastrous proportions.

12.1 - Luke 11:21-22; *12.2* - Proverbs 24:10

When I am weak

The beginning of your journey into being made strong by heaven is the acknowledgement of your weakness. There are no two ways about it; the weakness you don't acknowledge remains untreated and hidden under the veil of bold face. Acknowledgement here is not really unto man but unto your own self and unto God. Paul the apostle was a man of immense strength and power in the revelations of Christ but also a man who saw a weakness. Paul was able to appropriate divine strength in grace because he knew and acknowledged his need for it when he was weak. Hear what he had to say… *Therefore most gladly I will rather boast in my infirmities that the power of Christ may rest upon me. Therefore I take pleasure in distresses for Christ sake for when I am weak; then I am strong."* **[12.3]**. It is not faith not to acknowledge your limit, it is faith to acknowledge it and appropriate the limitless power of God therein and then go further. Stop explaining your weakness, flaws and limitations; acknowledge it and then a journey into help has begun. No one can be helped by heaven here on earth till you acknowledge your present status of need for help. As gracious as salvation in Christ is, no one gets saved until he or she sees the need to be saved from the world and its lost cause by the loving Saviour who died and rose again, even Jesus Christ the son of God.

Seek Help

Assumption in the kingdom of God is an express ticket to defeat. Don't assume strength, seek it. Seeking in the kingdom of God is as important as breathing is to life.

12.3 - Hebrews 12:9b-10

Even the things that God has promised or made available already in Christ are not thrown at people like pearls to pigs. Heaven's treasures are well kept only for seekers on earth. God said His plans for His people are good plans and not evil, but then must they seek Him with all of their hearts for the plans to find expression **[12.4]**. There are certain beneficial programmes the government of nations of the earth here put in place for their citizens year in year out. Some of these programmes are not automatically inclusive; one may need to register for some before access is granted. In same way, the programme of God for His people includes being strengthened against any flaw, shortcoming or infirmity. The registration of desire has to be submitted, or else weakness shall be perpetuated. David had much to say along this line, *"...Seek the lord and his strength; seek his face for ever more..."* **[12.5]**.

When Paul the Apostle, a kingdom champion extraordinaire saw a weakness in his life, he didn't just assume victory nor did he hope for victory. I have heard people say that they believe God for something and yet they do nothing about it. Idling and believing are not synonymous; faith without corresponding action is dead and inappropriate. Paul sought God three times, he stopped at number three not because the number of times meant anything. He stopped at number three because God had given him the response to his seeking and so he had proofs of strength now in the face of his weakness. If God had directed Paul to another man in whose hands God had put the help needed for the

12.4 - *Jeremiah 29:11-13;* ***12.5*** - *Psalms 105:4*

moment, he would have simply gone to the man. At times when we pray to God, He brings people in whose hands He has placed the strength we need our way. Kingdom champions must not be too proud to line up with such help and maximize the moment as ordained of God. When David was too weak to fight on one occasion and would have been killed by a Philistine, God didn't make him strong physical all of a sudden and turned him to an avatar of his heydays. God simply made him listen to wise counsel and step aside for a younger man who slayed the Philistine and saved the day.

Kingdom champions don't look up to man as their source of help, but at the same time don't turn their face away in pride from God-sent help through man.

Hide Your Weakness in Wisdom

Supernatural wisdom is a heritage of saints. It is un-saint-like to be void of wisdom and get stuck in life, not knowing left from right. Wisdom will help you with strength than ten mighty men in the city. So before seeking human companionship in your challenge, seek wisdom **[12.6]**. Wisdom is a defence; it makes you come across stronger than you probably are. If wisdom says flee in a situation, the wise thing is to flee, not to confront. If wisdom says let the weak say I am strong, it is not time to start explaining how you feel and how much you have tried. The word of God is the wisdom chess for the saints. It might sound outdated and unpopular, but happy are you when you settle down with it as the final authority in the issues of life **[12.7]**. Jesus said the secret of strength

12.6 - *Ecclesiastes 7:19;* **12.7** - *Matthew 7:24;*

against the storms of life is the wisdom of the word. When you make the word of God your wisdom, you have just plugged yourself into the wisdom behind the inspiration that wrote the word. Supposing the Bible is even the word of man and a compilation of men as many unbelievers argue, which it is not, (for it to have spanned such a long time, exerted such level of influence and drawn that level of global attention) it must have been written and inspired by men beyond mere men. If your business, career or whatever pursuits can enjoy the same level of success and influence, great shall you be called among men. Heeding the Bible as your wisdom chess is therefore a simple way to plug into the wisdom behind its inspiration and hiding your own weakness in the strength behind the inspiration and substance that has spanned ages. The bible has a lot to say about marriage, career, business, and pursuits of dreams. It has much to say about health, staying on top and at the cutting edge of life, and finding absolute all round fulfilment; but it takes plugging in to make the wisdom of God your hiding place **[12.8]**.

Put Your Strength to Work
Finally my reader, nothing works in the kingdom of champions until you work it. No one is a champion by mere saying or in proxy; we win in words and in deeds here. Stop waiting for someone to come and help you work it out; put your strength to work. After praying, Paul was not lying down weeping and waiting for something to happen. Whatever happened afterwards,

12.8 - *Psalms 119:99-100*

he made them happen. God had said sufficient grace had been released to Paul. Paul didn't say he felt the grace; he just took it raw as God said it and started running with it. We live in a feely-feeling age where everything is summarised in emotions and sensuality, but as a kingdom champion, you have to rise above such. Paul put the strength of God granted him to work immediately. The work started in his mouth, whenever he felt weakness, he started confessing strength that he had been given. He wasn't waiting again for a halo to appear, he just laid hold of the strength promised.

Having pastored for several years, I have come across believers who are in perpetual weakness, state of disadvantage and misfortune, even pre and post counselling, pre and post prayers, pre and post laying on of hands or even prophecy. One thing they all have in common is the romantic relationships they have with their weakness or challenges. They can't for once divorce the problem and take on what God has said or released in prayer or ministration. They are so helplessly attracted to the state of weakness and its attending pity and mourning with moaning that nothing else seems attractive to them than that wallowing. It is common for such to stop coming to church and go into a corner to lick wounds for some season and re-emerge in church to repeat the same cycle over and over again, world without end. Alternatively, they move from church to church and prophet to prophet, seeking stronger anointing and power whereas the one released for them last had gone to the shelf of dis-use where others that came before were also laid.

People labour in this kingdom to enter into rest. One of the labours is the labouring of putting your acquired strength from the Lord into use. It requires discipline, starting from the thoughts you give free reign in your heart, to the periscope through which you start seeing yourself and life through. As long as you keep seeing a weak loser that is not as lucky as others or a weakling that has no choice but to be put down and give in to oppression and depression, the strength in you will always elude you. Come out of dust, shake yourself up dear daughter of Zion; you are not weak because you are single. You can only be weak as much as you stay in weakness. Lose yourself from the self-inflicted band or the ones others are putting on your neck. Zion and captivity don't go together.

Start doing something with your strength. When Asa whom we saw in the lineage of David earlier on had acknowledged the present weakness and received the strength of the Lord in prayer, he didn't sit down and keep saying the same thing as before like a loser without hope [12.9]. Asa arose up and started smiting everything in a forward movement till he emerged triumphant as he should. Same can be said of Jehoshaphat in the same lineage of champions. He prayed, God heard and released strength, he started praising God in acknowledgement of answered prayers and he moved forward not backwards to take the spoils of war of the enemies smitten of the Lord. The strength of God in you will only manifest to the

12.9 - *2 Chronicles 14:12-15*

level to which you put it into use.

God is infinite, we are not, but we can go really far in the infinity of God and do great exploits in His strength till we make our strength infinite in Him too. At that stage we can boldly say like Paul, that we are doing all things through Christ who is strengthening us.

Be made strong in the strength of the Lord and remain strong all the way.

Shalom.

www.ingramcontent.com/pod-product-compliance
Lightning Source LLC
Chambersburg PA
CBHW061329040426
42444CB00011B/2826